Creating Mobile Apps with jQuery Mobile

Learn to make practical, unique, real-world sites that span a variety of industries and technologies with the world's most popular mobile development library

Shane Gliser

[PACKT] open source✳
community experience distilled
PUBLISHING

BIRMINGHAM - MUMBAI

Creating Mobile Apps with jQuery Mobile

First published: April 2013

Production Reference: 1170413

Published by Packt Publishing Ltd.
Livery Place
35 Livery Street
Birmingham B3 2PB, UK

ISBN 978-1-78216-006-9

www.packtpub.com

Cover Image by Asher Wishkerman (wishkerman@hotmail.com)

Credits

Author
Shane Gliser

Reviewers
Mario Agüero

Kaiser Ahmed

Andy Matthews

Tony Pye

Acquisition Editor
Usha Iyer

Lead Technical Editor
Arun Nadar

Technical Editors
Jalasha D'costa

Soumya Kanti

Ishita Malhi

Varun Pius Rodrigues

Project Coordinators
Anish Ramchandani

Navu Dhillon

Proofreaders
Lauren Tobon

Elinor Perry-Smith

Indexer
Rekha Nair

Production Coordinator
Pooja Chiplunkar

Cover Work
Pooja Chiplunkar

About the Author

Shane Gliser graduated from Washburn University in 2001, specializing in Java development. Over the next several years, he developed a love of web development and taught himself HTML, CSS, and JavaScript. Having shifted his focus again, Shane's primary passions are user experience and the mobile web.

Shane began working with jQuery Mobile while it was still in the Alpha 2 phase and deployed American Century Investments' mobile site while the framework was still in Beta 2. Since then, he has rebranded and re-launched his own personal business, Roughly Brilliant Digital Studios (`http://roughlybrilliant.com`), as a place where he could start blogging tips about using jQuery Mobile.

Major thanks go to Todd Parker, Scott Jehl, and the rest of the crew at Filament Group and the many other volunteers who have given their time and talent to creating jQuery Mobile.

Jim Tharp, thank you for being my mobile partner-in-crime and for your continuous, epic sense of humor.

To the leadership team at American Century Investments, thank you for believing in my little two-week demo and trusting us to march down this unknown path.

About the Reviewers

Mario Agüero is a Software Engineer from Costa Rica with a long experience in both software development and academics.

He has developed several backend engines for clients and directed the adoption of best practices for growing business. From the last couple of years, he has also been working in frontend development, developing great interfaces and components for his clients' websites.

He has the advantage of being strongly agnostic about platforms, making him one of the few persons recognized as an excellent instructor and architect in both .NET and Java.

On the academic side, he has always been ahead in actively promoting technologies such as XML, JavaScript, and JSON before they became mainstream. He has helped with and developed several training programs for professional updates and career changes.

He has also reviewed the Spanish editions of several books, such as *PHP for Dummies*.

Kaiser Ahmed is a professional web developer. He has acquired his Bachelor of Science degree from Khulna University of Engineering and Technology (KUET) and his Master of Science degree in Computer Science Engineering from United International University, Dhaka. He is a cofounder of CyberXpress.Net, Inc. (www.cyberxpress.net), which is based in Bangladesh.

He has been working as Senior Software Developer at Krembo Interactive and D1SH. COM CORP., Canada, for 2 years.

He has a wide array of technical skills, knowledge of the Web, and experience across a spectrum of online-development activities in building and improving online properties, which he has done for multiple clients. He enjoys creating site architecture and infrastructure; backend development using open source technologies such as PHP, MySQL, Apache, Linux, and others (for example, LAMP); and frontend development using CSS and HTML/XHTML.

I want to thank my loving wife, Maria Akther, for her great support.

Andy Matthews has been working as a web and application developer for over 16 years, with experience in a wide range of industries and a skillset which includes UI/UX, graphic design, and programming. He has co-authored the book *jQuery Mobile Web Development Essentials*, and writes for online publications such as NetTuts and .NET Magazine. He is a frequent speaker at conferences around the USA, and he has developed software for the open source community including several of the most popular jQuery Mobile projects on the web. He blogs at `andyMatthews.net`, he tweets at `@commadelimited`. He lives in Nashville, Tennessee with his wife and four children.

Tony Pye has over 10 years of experience in producing web-based solutions, and strives to stay ahead when it comes to rapidly-evolving web technologies in order to be able to offer innovative solutions.

He is passionate about matching business goals with innovative use of technology. As the head of Digital Production at INK Digital Agency, he has been guiding clients through the complex digital world; integrating digital marketing with internal business systems is his specialty.

Liaising with members from the creative and user-experience teams, meeting clients, presenting ideas, and helping define goals are just a part of Tony's normal day at INK.

Some of the solutions he has helped produce have delivered exciting results for companies including Ballymore, Morrisons, Renault, Tarmac, Aviva, LA fitness, and the University of Leeds.

Tony has also worked on a number of other books as the technical reviewer, which include Pro HTML5 Programming and The Definitive Guide to HTML5 WebSocket (not yet published).

I'd like to thank my beautiful wife for her support and patience during the long nights I've worked. Her fantastic coffee-making skills were certainly put to great use. Thanks darling!!

www.PacktPub.com

Support files, eBooks, discount offers and more

You might want to visit www.PacktPub.com for support files and downloads related to your book.

Did you know that Packt offers eBook versions of every book published, with PDF and ePub files available? You can upgrade to the eBook version at www.PacktPub.com and as a print book customer, you are entitled to a discount on the eBook copy. Get in touch with us at service@packtpub.com for more details.

At www.PacktPub.com, you can also read a collection of free technical articles, sign up for a range of free newsletters and receive exclusive discounts and offers on Packt books and eBooks.

http://PacktLib.PacktPub.com

Do you need instant solutions to your IT questions? PacktLib is Packt's online digital book library. Here, you can access, read and search across Packt's entire library of books.

Why Subscribe?

- Fully searchable across every book published by Packt
- Copy and paste, print and bookmark content
- On demand and accessible via web browser

Free Access for Packt account holders

If you have an account with Packt at www.PacktPub.com, you can use this to access PacktLib today and view nine entirely free books. Simply use your login credentials for immediate access.

To my wonderful wife, Laney. Yes, now I will finally finish the basement.

Table of Contents

Preface   1

Chapter 1: Prototyping jQuery Mobile   9

The game has changed   9
The mobile usage pattern   10
HTML prototyping versus drawing   11
Getting our hands dirty with small business   12
  The rest of the site   15
Requirements   18
  Alternates to paper prototyping   19
Summary   19

Chapter 2: A Mom-and-Pop Mobile Website   21

A new jQuery Mobile boilerplate   21
  Meta viewport differences   23
  Full-site links beyond the industry standard   24
The global JavaScript   26
  .live versus .on   27
The global CSS   28
Breaking the HTML into a server side template   28
What we need to create our site   31
  Getting Glyphish and defining custom icons   32
Linking to phones, e-mails, and maps   34
  Custom fonts   37
  Page curl shadow effects for our list items   38
  Optimization: why you should be thinking of it first   39
  The final product   41
  The custom CSS   42
The resulting first page   47

Getting the user to our mobile site   48
  Detecting and redirecting using JavaScript   49
  Detecting on the server   51
Summary   51

Chapter 3: Analytics, long forms, and frontend validation   53
Google Static Maps   53
  Adding Google Analytics   55
Long and multi-page forms   60
Integrating jQuery Validate   62
E-commerce tracking with Google Analytics   72
Summary   74

**Chapter 4: QR Codes, Geolocation, Google Maps API,
and HTML5 Video   75**
QR codes   76
Geolocation   77
Integrating the Google Maps API   87
Geek-out moment—GPS monitoring   92
Linking and embedding video   98
Summary   100

**Chapter 5: Client-side Templating, JSON APIs, and HTML5
Web Storage   101**
Client-side templating   102
Patching into JSON APIs (Twitter)   104
Programmatically changing pages   113
Generated pages and DOM weight management   113
Leveraging RSS feeds   114
  Forcing responsive images   119
HTML5 Web Storage   119
  Browser-based databases (a work in progress)   120
  JSON to the rescue   120
Leveraging the Google Feeds API   122
Summary   124

Chapter 6: HTML5 Audio   125
HTML5 Audio   126
Fixed position persistent toolbars (really!?)   128
Controlling HTML5 Audio with JavaScript   130
HTML5 Audio in iOS is different   136
The all-in-one solution (multipage made useful)   136
Saving to the home screen with HTML5 manifest   150
Summary   152

Chapter 7: Fully Responsive Photography — **153**

Creating a basic gallery using PhotoSwipe — **154**

Supporting the full range of device sizes – responsive web design — **156**

Text readability and responsive design — **161**

Smartphone-sized devices — 164

Tablet-sized devices — 165

Desktop-sized devices — 166

Cycling background images — **166**

Another responsive approach – RESS — **169**

The final code — **170**

Summary — **170**

Chapter 8: Integrating jQuery Mobile into Existing Sites — **171**

Detecting mobile – server-side, client-side, and the combination of the two — **171**

Browser sniffing versus feature detection — 172

WURFL – server-side database-driven browser sniffing — 172

JavaScript-based browser sniffing — 177

JavaScript-based feature detection using Modernizr — 178

JavaScript-based lean feature detection — 179

Server-side plus client-side detection — 179

Mobilizing full-site pages – the hard way — **183**

Know your role — 183

Step 1 of 2 – focus on content, marketing cries foul! — 184

Step 2 of 2 – choose global navigation style and insert — 185

Global nav as a separate page — 185

Global nav at the bottom — 186

Global nav as a panel — 187

The hard way – final thoughts — 187

Mobilizing full-site pages – the easy way — **187**

Summary — **194**

Chapter 9: Content Management Systems and jQM — **195**

The current CMS landscape — **196**

WordPress and jQuery Mobile — **196**

Manually installing the mobile theme switcher — 198

Automatically installing the mobile theme switcher — 198

Configuring the mobile theme switcher — 199

Drupal and jQuery Mobile — 200

Updating your WordPress and Drupal templates — **205**

WordPress – Golden Apples jQM Theme — 205

Drupal – jQuery Mobile Theme — 205

Adobe Experience Manager	**206**
Summary	**208**
Chapter 10: Putting It All Together – Flood.FM	**209**
A Taste of Balsamiq	**210**
Organizing your code	**212**
MVC, MVVM, MV*	212
MV* and jQuery Mobile	213
The application	214
The events	215
The model	216
Introduction to the Web Audio API	**217**
Prompting the user to install your app	**220**
New device-level hardware access	**222**
Accelerometers	222
Camera	222
APIs on the horizon	223
To app or not to app, that is the question	**223**
Raining on the parade (take this seriously)	223
Three good reasons for compiling an app	225
The project itself IS the product	225
Access to native-only hardware capabilities	225
Push notifications	225
Supporting current customers	225
PhoneGap versus Apache Cordova	**226**
Summary	**229**
Index	**231**

Preface

Can we build it? Yes, we can!

Mobile is the fastest growing technology sector in existence. It is a wave of change that has shattered all analysts' expectations. You have the choice to harness that wave or to be swept under. In *Creating Mobile Apps with jQuery Mobile*, we'll take you through several projects of increasing complexity across a variety of industries. At the same time, we'll tackle several mobile usability and experience issues that are common to all mobile implementations, not just jQuery Mobile.

By the end you will have all the skills necessary to take jQuery Mobile and a host of other technologies and techniques to create truly unique offerings. This will be fun. It will be challenging, and by the end, you will be quoting Bob the Builder, "Can we build it? Yes we can!"

What this book covers

Chapter 1, Prototyping jQuery Mobile, harnesses the power of rapid prototyping before you start coding. Come to a quicker, better, and shared understanding with your clients.

Chapter 2, A Mom-and-Pop Mobile Website, implements the prototypes from *Chapter 1*. The design is unique and begins to establish a base server-side template.

Chapter 3, Analytics, Long Forms, and Front-end Validation, takes the casual implementation of *Chapter 2* and adds in Google Analytics, the jQuery Validate framework, and a technique for dealing with long forms.

Chapter 4, QR Codes, Geolocation, Google Maps API, and HTML5 Video, will have you implement a site for a movie theater chain.

Chapter 5, Client-side Templating, JSON APIs, and HTML5 Web Storage, creates a social news nexus, tapping into the API powers of Twitter, Flickr, and the Google Feeds API.

Chapter 6, HTML5 Audio, takes HTML5 audio and progressive enhancement to turn a very basic web audio player page into a musical artist's showcase.

Chapter 7, Fully Responsive Photography, explores the user of jQuery Mobile as a mobile-first, **responsive web design (RWD)** platform. We also take a very quick look at typography as it applies to RWD.

Chapter 8, Integrating jQuery Mobile into Existing Sites, explores the methods of building jQuery Mobile sites for clients who want their pages mobilized but don't have a **content management system (CMS)**. We also dig deep into mobile detection methods including client-side, server-side, and a combination of the two.

Chapter 9, Content Management Systems and jQM, teaches us how to integrate jQM into WordPress and Drupal.

Chapter 10, Putting it all together – Flood.FM, builds on the knowledge of the previous chapters and creates, adds a little more, and considers compilation using PhoneGap Build.

What you need for this book

You really only need a few things for this book.

- A text editor

  All you need is a basic text editor for your code; Notepad++ is great on Windows. I really like Sublime Text 2. Eclipse will work though it's a bit heavy-handed. Dreamweaver is pretty good but pricey. It really doesn't matter much; you can pick whatever text editor makes you happy.

- A web server

  You could use a hosted solution such as HostGator, Godaddy, 1&1, and many more, or keep all your testing local using something like XAMPP, WAMP, MAMP, or LAMP on your development box.

- JavaScript libraries

  Here and there in the chapters we'll introduce a few JS libraries. In each case, I'll tell you what they are and where to find them.

- A developer's sense of humor

  We all think of it, we all say it. You'll find a rant or two in here. Take them for what they're worth and never too seriously.

Who this book is for

If you are already fairly good with web development (HTML, CSS, JavaScript, and jQuery), that's good enough for me. You can pick up jQM along the way in this book and I think you'll be fine.

What we will cover

- Ideation and prototyping techniques
- Integrating custom fonts and icon sets
- Integrating client-side form validation using jQuery Validate
- Google Analytics, Maps, and Feeds APIs
- Geo location
- Embedding HTML5 Video and Audio
- Using client-side templates and JSON
- Digesting RSS feeds
- Integrating PhotoSwipe
- Media queries
- Mobile detection techniques
- Integrating with Wordpress and Drupal
- Integrating with pre-existing sites

Why jQuery Mobile

Kings rise and fall so fast in the mobile sector that it's almost impossible to predict who and what will win. Just ask RIM (makers of BlackBerry devices) who went from total domination down to 6 percent of the world's market share. With this level and speed of change, how can you know that you are choosing the right platform for your projects?

- **A safe bet**

    The core jQuery library is used on over 57 percent of all websites in existence and the growth rate shows no signs of slowing. (`http://trends.builtwith.com/javascript/jQuery`). It is, by far, the most trusted name in open source JavaScript libraries. Now that they have tossed their hat into the mobile ring, you can bet that jQuery Mobile is a pretty safe choice for reaching the most people with the smallest effort.

It is also worth noting that you will probably move on from most of your projects after a time. Using jQM will increase the likelihood that whoever comes after you will already have the skill set to pick up where you left off.

- **Broadest device support**

  jQuery Mobile has the broadest range of device support. This has always been part of their mission through their exceptional adherence to **progressive enhancement (PE)**. When an escalator breaks, it does not become completely useless. It becomes simply stairs. In the same way, jQuery Mobile does some really awesome things for those who have smartphones. But what about the rest? They will see a standard web page without all the bells and whistles. At the end of the day, a well-crafted jQM page can work for everyone.

- **Mobile-first but not mobile-only**

  jQM was designed from the ground up with mobile in mind but with some judicious use of **responsive web design (RWD),** a single jQM project can service mobile, tablet, and even desktop.

- **Declarative, not programmatic**

  Most of what you want to do in jQM can be done without writing a single line of code. This makes it an ideal tool for even the newest of newbs to jump in and get their feet wet in the mobile space. Designers with no real programming experience can easily turn their visions into skinned, working prototypes. For those of us who can program, it means that there is much less coding we need to do and that is always a good thing. jQM perfectly fits the jQuery core motto of "write less, do more."

- **jQM versus other frameworks**

  There are many choices for your consideration if you want to use a mobile framework. Check out `http://www.markus-falk.com/mobile-frameworks-comparison-chart/` for a breakdown tool comparing all the options. The bottom line is this: if you want to support everybody and do it easily, jQuery Mobile is the right choice of framework.

- **jQM versus responsive web design**

  Much is being said these days about RWD. I'm all for it. A single unified site is every developer's dream. However, this usually requires that the website be built from the ground up with RWD in mind. This also presumes that every page of the site is worth serving to a mobile audience. If you ever have such a growth opportunity, enjoy it.

The sad truth is, most of the rest of us don't get the luxury of starting a whole new site from scratch, nor the time and tripled budget to do the job right. And, if we're being quite honest… many sites have a lot of useless pages that have no business being in the ultra-focused, task-oriented, get-in-get-out-world that is the mobile web. You know it. I know it. A custom crafted solution that perfectly fits the users' needs and context is usually a better way to go.

- **jQM versus rolling your own**

  You certainly could choose to roll out your own mobile sites from scratch but that would be tantamount to felling a forest with an axe so you could make the boards to build your own house. You are no less of a craftsman for using premade components to make your masterpiece. Mobile frameworks exist for a reason, the amount of development time and cross-device testing that goes into them will save you more time and headaches than you can fathom.

  It is worth noting that two out of the three top industry leaders highlighted in Kasina's report, *Mobile Leadership for Asset Managers and Insurers* (`http://www.kasina.com/Page.asp?ID=1415`), were crafted using jQuery Mobile. Franklin Templeton, American Century Investments, and Vanguard were highlighted. The first two were implemented using jQM.

  Full disclosure: I was part of the team that created the referenced version of the mobile site for American Century Investment so I'm rather proud of this report.

Progressive enhancement and graceful degradation

Resistance is futile. It is going to happen to you. Every year there are new exploits announced at the Black Hat conferences (`http://www.blackhat.com/`). Just like clockwork, companies neuter their smartphone users by turning off JavaScript until a patch can be provided. One or more people within your mobile audience will be affected.

While this situation can be almost as annoying as early editions of Internet Explorer, jQuery Mobile can help, thanks to its masterful use of progressive enhancement. If you have coded your pages in accordance with the framework's design then you will have nothing to fear by the loss of JavaScript. The site will still work. It may not be as pretty, but it will function for everyone from the smartest of smartphones to the dumbest of "dumbphones".

It is our responsibility (as distasteful as it may be) to test our offerings with JavaScript turned off to ensure that people can always access our product. It is not hard to flip the settings on our phones and just take a look at what happens. Frequently, it's trivial to fix whatever is wrong.

All that being said, we are going to *mercilessly* break that rule in this book because we are going beyond the basics of the framework. When possible, we will try to keep this principle in mind and provide fallback alternatives but some of what we are going to try just can't be done without JavaScript. Welcome to the twenty-first century!

Accessibility

Smartphones are excellent tools for those with accessibility needs. The jQuery Mobile team has made every effort to support the W3C's WAI-ARIA standards for accessibility. At the very least, you should test your finished product with your phone's voice assist technologies. You will be shocked at just how well your site can perform. Your customers who need the help with be thrilled.

Conventions

In this book, you will find a number of styles of text that distinguish between different kinds of information. Here are some examples of these styles, and an explanation of their meaning.

Code words in text are shown as follows: "To use the manifest file, your web server or `.htaccess` will have to be configured to return the type of `text/cache-manifest`."

A block of code is set as follows:

```
<link rel="apple-touch-icon-precomposed" sizes="144x144" href="images/
album144.png">
<link rel="apple-touch-icon-precomposed" sizes="114x114" href="images/
album114.png">
<link rel="apple-touch-icon-precomposed" sizes="72x72" href="images/
album72.png">
<link rel="apple-touch-icon-precomposed" href="images/album57.png">
```

New terms and **important words** are shown in bold. Words that you see on the screen, in menus or dialog boxes for example, appear in the text like this: "From there you can download the latest copy of **WURFL API package** and unzip it."

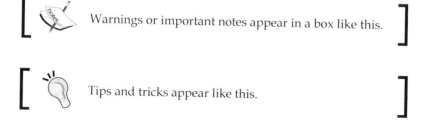

Warnings or important notes appear in a box like this.

Tips and tricks appear like this.

Reader feedback

Feedback from our readers is always welcome. Let us know what you think about this book—what you liked or may have disliked. Reader feedback is important for us to develop titles that you really get the most out of.

To send us general feedback, simply send an e-mail to feedback@packtpub.com, and mention the book title through the subject of your message.

If there is a topic that you have expertise in and you are interested in either writing or contributing to a book, see our author guide on www.packtpub.com/authors.

Customer support

Now that you are the proud owner of a Packt book, we have a number of things to help you to get the most from your purchase.

Downloading the color images of this book

We also provide you with a PDF file that has color images of the screenshots/diagrams used in this book. The color images will help you better understand the chapters.You can download this file from http://www.packtpub.com/sites/default/files/downloads/0069_images.pdf.

Downloading the example code

You can download the example code files for all Packt books you have purchased from your account at http://www.packtpub.com. If you purchased this book elsewhere, you can visit http://www.packtpub.com/support and register to have the files e-mailed directly to you.

Errata

Although we have taken every care to ensure the accuracy of our content, mistakes do happen. If you find a mistake in one of our books—maybe a mistake in the text or the code—we would be grateful if you would report this to us. By doing so, you can save other readers from frustration and help us improve subsequent versions of this book. If you find any errata, please report them by visiting http://www.packtpub.com/support, selecting your book, clicking on the **errata submission form** link, and entering the details of your errata. Once your errata are verified, your submission will be accepted and the errata will be uploaded to our website, or added to any list of existing errata, under the Errata section of that title.

Piracy

Piracy of copyright material on the Internet is an ongoing problem across all media. At Packt, we take the protection of our copyright and licenses very seriously. If you come across any illegal copies of our works, in any form, on the Internet, please provide us with the location address or website name immediately so that we can pursue a remedy.

Please contact us at copyright@packtpub.com with a link to the suspected pirated material.

We appreciate your help in protecting our authors, and our ability to bring you valuable content.

Questions

You can contact us at questions@packtpub.com if you are having a problem with any aspect of the book, and we will do our best to address it.

1

Prototyping jQuery Mobile

On November 22, 2011, I started my blog at `RoughlyBrilliant.com` as a way to share everything I was learning about jQuery Mobile and Mobile UX (user experience). I had no idea what it would turn into and what would strike a chord. Since it's a developer-centric blog, it came as a bit of a surprise to me that the remarks I made about stepping away from the keyboard and sketching our designs first would spark the most positive comments. It is my firm belief that the best way to start your jQuery Mobile projects, is on a pad of Post-it notes.

There is a good chance that this chapter will feel like the most work and feel the most foreign. But ultimately, I believe it will probably be the chapter that gives you the most growth. It's normal for developers to sit down and start coding, but it's time to grow past that. It is time to step away from the keyboard!

In this chapter, we cover:

- The changing mobile playing field
- The mobile usage pattern
- Paper prototyping
- Key components for a small business mobile site
- Drawing the jQuery Mobile UI
- Other prototyping methods

The game has changed

There was a time, not so long ago, when developers could make a product and people would use it no matter how bad it was. It would generally garner some level of success simply by virtue of its existence. We now live in an age where there is a lot more competition. Now, with tools like jQuery Mobile, anyone can quickly craft impressive-looking mobile sites in a matter of hours.

So, how do we differentiate ourselves from the competition? We could certainly compete on price. People love a good value. But there is something that has always seemed to trump price and that is the user's experience. **User experience (UX)** is what differentiates most of the world's most successful brands.

Which computer company is not only staying afloat but is absolutely swimming in success? Apple. This may be partially due to the fact that their products cost three times what they should. Ultimately, I believe it is because they've always been on the forefront of designing around the user.

Amazon provides a great experience by helping you find what you're looking for quickly. They give great reviews and recommendations for your purchasing decisions. Their one-click purchase is so handy that they've actually fought in court to protect it as a competition point (`http://en.wikipedia.org/wiki/1-Click`).

Google could have gone the way of Yahoo, AOL, MSN, and so many others. They could have promoted whatever they wanted on their homepage. Instead, they have kept their homepage almost as clean as the day they started. They have their name, a search box, and great results. At most, there's some cute rendering of their logo. They give the user what they want and pretty much stay out of the way.

It's hard! We like to think that how we make a program or web page is crucial. We like to think that, by shaving off 10 percent of our code, we're making a big difference. But have you ever tried to explain the details of your current project to a friend and just watched their eyes glaze over? Nobody cares but us. All they hear is faster, smaller, easier, simpler, and so on. They only care about things that directly bear on their life, their user experience.

The most important lesson we can learn as developers is that we can write the most elegant code, create the most efficient systems, accomplish small miracles in less than 1K of JavaScript, but if we fail in the area of usability... we will fail completely.

The mobile usage pattern

jQuery Mobile is not a magic bullet. It will not create an instant magnetism to our products. Technologies and libraries will not save us if we fail to realize the environment and usage patterns of our users.

Think about this: when was the last time you spent more than three continuous minutes on any one site or app on your phone that wasn't a game? We all know how addictive Angry Birds can be but, aside from that, we tend to be in-and-out in a hurry. The nature of mobile usage is short bursts of efficient activity. This is because our smartphones are the perfect time reclamation devices. We whip them out wherever we have a spare minute including:

- Around the house (recipes, texting, boredom)

- While waiting in lines or waiting rooms (boredom)

- Shopping (women: deal hunting, men: boredom)

- During work (meetings, bathroom-we've all done it)

- Watching TV (every commercial break)

- Commuting (riding mass transit or stuck in traffic jams)

We can easily see the microburst activity through our own daily lives. This is the environment that we have to tailor our products to if we hope to succeed. Above all else, this will require us to focus. What did the user come to us to do while they are waiting in line? What can they accomplish in a single commercial break? What task would they consider number one during their number two?

HTML prototyping versus drawing

Do NOT start with the code. Being a developer, this is really hard to say. jQuery Mobile is very fast and easy. Refactoring is also very fast. However, there is something that happens when you jump right into HTML prototyping.

People who don't know code will assume that we're much closer to a complete product than we actually may be. This is especially true with jQuery Mobile because even the most rudimentary stab at a project comes out looking polished and complete.

People will start to fixate on minutia like spacing, margins, colors, logo size, and so on.

Due to the sunk cost of our time in the current design, we are less likely to make significant changes from whatever we initial coded because refactoring is easier than a do-over.

Instead, get a pen and paper. *Wait, what?* Isn't this a web developer book? Relax, you don't have to be an artist. Trust the process. There will be plenty of opportunities to code later. For now, we are going to draw our first jQuery Mobile site.

The great thing about starting with paper-based ideation is:

- We are more willing to simply throw out a drawing that took less than 30 seconds to create

- Actually sketching by hand uses a different part of the brain and unlocks our creative centers

- We can come up with three completely different designs in the time it takes to create one HTML page

- Everyone can contribute their best ideas even if they're not skilled in graphic design or coding

- We will naturally begin by drawing the most important things first

- More attention is paid to the ideas and flows that actually make our site work instead of the myriad details, which few would even notice

- We will probably end up with a more user-centered design since we're drawing what we would actually want

Ideally, 3x5 Post-its notes are perfect because we can easily lay them out on walls or tables to simulate site structure or process flows. We could even use them to conduct usability testing. A little later, we'll lay out our drawing for the owner to see how the whole thing could work before we get buyoff.

Getting our hands dirty with small business

According to Katherine Kobe at `http://archive.sba.gov/advo/research/rs299tot.pdf`:

> *"Small businesses continue to play a vital role in the economy of the United States. During the 1998-2004 time period, small businesses produced half of private nonfarm GDP."*

An article at `http://www.msnbc.msn.com/id/16872553/` says:

> *"While some two-thirds of small firms make it past the two-year mark, just 44 percent can hack it for four years, according to the latest data from the Bureau of Labor Statistics."*

Even in the land of big business, it bodes well for our craft; there is such a volume and churn of small businesses. That means an almost endless supply of mom-and-pop shops that are trying to compete. That's where we come in.

Nicky's Pizza has recently opened its doors. Like so many other businesses, the owner realized that he should have a website before it opens the doors. His friend made the website and it's actually pretty good. It's just not mobile yet.

The pizza is great and while we sit there enjoying, we bust out a pen and grab a napkin. We are about to make a mobile website right here, right now, and win some business. Let's get started.

For any small, local business there are certain staples that should probably be first and foremost on their mobile site:

- Location
- Contact information
- Services/goods provided

Since this is a restaurant, services will be the menu. They also were smart enough to create a Facebook page. So, we'll link to that and bring in some testimonials.

Since we're drawing and not using a tool, you can choose to be as detailed as you like. The following figures are two examples of drawing the same page. Either works to communicate the core ideas.

When working with our own team, the first is probably just enough since we all know what jQuery Mobile can do. We know what details the framework will fill in and can draw just enough to tell each other what we're thinking. However, when drawing for customers (or people who you know are more visual and detail-oriented), we would do well to take the few extra seconds to add the finer details like shadows, gradient shading, and, especially, the logo. Business owners are very proud of their babies, and your effort to include it will instantly grant your drawing that little bit of extra gravity.

The first is certainly good enough to pick up, hold in the hand, and pretend it's a smartphone screen. In the second figure, we can see how much difference actually drawing out the logo can make and how adding harder edges and shadows give a sense of depth. A little polish goes a long way.

There are several ways to go about adding drop shadows to your drawings. The most artistic way is to use pencil but the problem with drawing in pencil is that it leads to smudging, and paying too much attention to fine detail. These drawings are supposed to be rough. If you screw up slightly, no big deal. After all, you've probably spent less than a minute on each drawing and that's the idea. The goal is to get to a shared, visual understanding quickly.

Here are four different ways to draw the same button: pencil, pen, Sharpie, and markers. My personal preference is to use a fine point Sharpie.

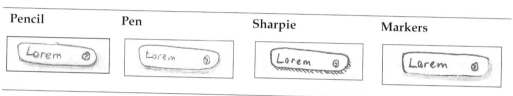

Here are some other jQuery Mobile elements and ways to draw them:

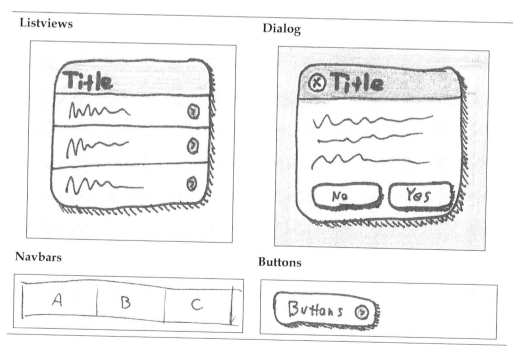

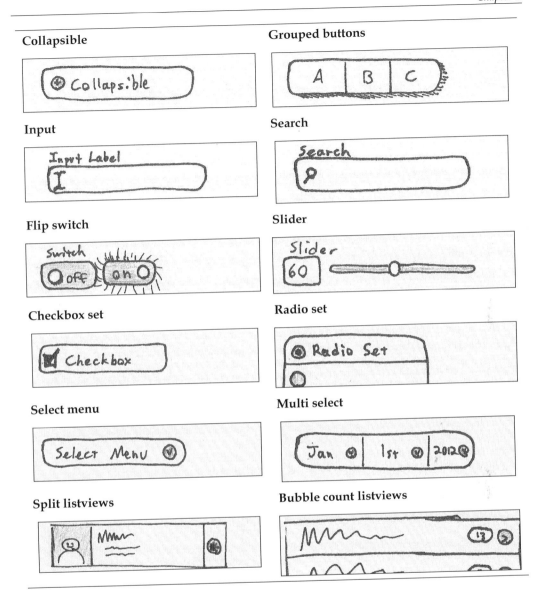

Collapsible

⊕ Collapsible

Grouped buttons

A | B | C

Input

Input Label

Search

Search
🔍

Flip switch

Switch
Off | on

Slider

Slider
60

Checkbox set

☑ Checkbox

Radio set

◉ Radio Set
◯

Select menu

Select Menu ✓

Multi select

Jan ⊗ | 1st ⊗ | 2012 ⊗

Split listviews

Bubble count listviews

12 ⊛

The rest of the site

The Map It button will lead the user to this page where we will list the address and have a static Google map. Clicking on either the address or the map will link to the full Google Maps location.

On Android and iOS 5 systems, linking to Google Maps will cause the native system to bring up the specified location in the native interface which will allow for turn-by-turn navigation. That changed in iOS 6 but we'll get to that later.

As an added bonus, in case users don't want to go to the physical location, let's throw a telephone link on the button labeled `Call for delivery.`

Note the different thicknesses of lines. Also, a touch of color and our typical drop shadows. Adding these little details are not particularly hard and can make a big difference.

All of the `Call` buttons throughout the site will launch the native call interface. The next drawing is of the iOS view of a call dialog. Android is pretty similar.

Notice the little shiney lines on the button in the background indicating that it was clicked. Notice also, the way that we've shaded out the background (pencil work) to indicate it's modal status.

Now, let's consider the menu and what will serve as a global header. The first two links that you put into the global header will be turned into buttons. There is a setting to auto-insert a back button in the place we currently have the home button. Just add `data-add-back-btn="true"` to the jQuery Mobile page. However, I generally wouldn't use this. Usability testing that I've helped to facilitate shows that most people simply push their device's native back buttons. So, let's make our first link `Home`, the second link as `Call`.

Here we see the detail view for salads. It's pretty much the same as before but we've done some formatting within the list views. We'll see the actual code for that in the next chapter.

Naturally, we could use a whiteboard and markers to do all this work. We can collaboratively draw our ideas on the board and take snapshots with the very smartphones we intend to target. My recommendation is to use our faithful Post-it notes and simply stick them to the whiteboard and use the markers to indicate screen flows. The following figure shows how my board looked after mapping out the project:

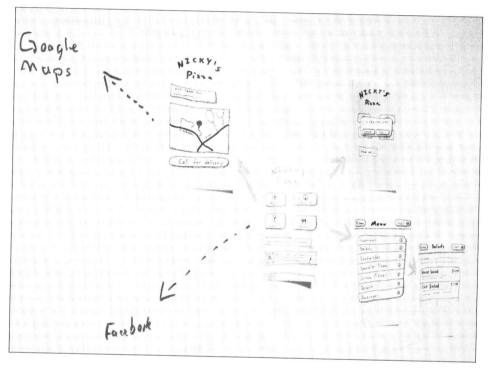

If we need to remap our application flows, all we have to do is shuffle the notes and redraw our lines. It's a lot less work than redrawing everything a few feet farther down the whiteboard.

Requirements

Consider what we've laid out so far. Considering the screens we've drawn and the fact that the owner was able to view and sign-off that this is what he wants, how many more questions are there to ask? Do we really need some Excel document listing out requirements or a 30-page **Functional Design Spec (FDS)** document to tell you exactly what everything is supposed to be and do? Wouldn't this be enough? Does it have to really be done in Photoshop and produced as a slide deck?

Consider also that what we have done so far has cost us a grand total of five Post-its, one Sharpie, one pencil, and 20 minutes. I believe the case here has been abundantly made that for most sites, this is all you need and you can do it yourself.

Alternates to paper prototyping

If the speed and simplicity of paper prototyping are not enough to convince you to step away from the keyboard, then consider two other options for rapid prototyping:

- **Balsamiq Mockups** (`http://www.balsamiq.com/`)
- **Axure RP** (`http://www.axure.com/`)

I personally recommend Balsamiq Mockups. The prototypes it produces have a uniform but hand-drawn look. This will accomplish the same thing as paper prototyping but with more consistent output and easier collaboration across distributed teams. Both of these tools can produce fully-interactive mockups, as well allow the user to actually click through the prototype. Ultimately, paper prototyping is still faster and anyone can contribute.

Summary

For those of us who have never encountered paper prototyping as a serious discipline, this can feel very weird at first. With any luck, the lessons learned here have expanded your mind and given you a new zeal for crafting a good user experience. If you would like to delve deeper into ideation techniques, the best book I can recommend on the topic is *Gamestorming* by Dave Gary (`http://www.goodreads.com/book/show/9364936-gamestorming`).

You should now be able to effectively sketch a jQuery Mobile interface for both your colleagues and customers. In the next chapter, we'll translate what was drawn here into a real jQuery Mobile implementation that goes beyond the normal jQuery Mobile look and feel. Just remember, the user experience and usability come first. Go for quick, focused bursts of intuitive productivity.

2
A Mom-and-Pop Mobile Website

The previous chapter taught us some valuable lessons about paper prototyping and gave us a solid ground on which to start our development. Now, we will take those drawings and turn them into an actual jQuery Mobile (jQM) site that acts responsively and looks unique.

In this chapter, we cover:

- A new jQuery Mobile boilerplate
- A new way of thinking about full-site links
- Breaking the boilerplate into a configurable server-side PHP template
- Using alternate icon sets
- Custom fonts
- Page curl effects using only CSS
- Performance optimization tips
- Mobile detection and redirection techniques

A new jQuery Mobile boilerplate

The jQuery Mobile docs have a lot of hidden gems. They make a great starting point but there are actually several ways of doing your base template. There is single-page template, multipage template, templates with global configuration, and dynamically-generated pages.

So, let's start out with a new jQM single-page boilerplate based on the original single-page template (`http://view.jquerymobile.com/1.3.0/docs/widgets/pages/`). We will evolve this as we move into other chapters so it becomes an all-encompassing template. Following is the basic directory structure we'll create for this chapter and the files we'll use:

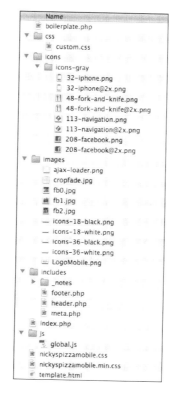

For now, here is the base HTML. Let's store it in `template.html`:

```
<!DOCTYPE html>
<html>

<head>
    <meta charset="utf-8">
    <meta name="viewport" content="width=device-width, initial-scale=1, maximum-scale=1.0, user-scalable=no">
```

```
    <link rel="stylesheet" href="http://code.jquery.com/mobile/1.1.0/
jquery.mobile-1.1.0.min.css" />
    <link rel="stylesheet" href="css/custom.css" />
    <script src="http://code.jquery.com/jquery-1.7.1.min.js"></script>
    <script src="js/custom-scripting.js"></script>
    <script src="http://code.jquery.com/mobile/1.1.0/jquery.mobile-
1.1.0.min.js"></script>
    <title>Boilerplate</title>
</head>
<body>
    <div data-role="page">
        <div data-role="header">
            <h1>Boilerplate</h1>
        </div>
        <div data-role="content">
            <p>Page Body content</p>
        </div>
        <div data-role="footer">
            <h4>Footer content</h4>
        </div>
        <a href="{dynamic location}" class="fullSiteLink">
View Full Site</a>
    </div>
</body>
</html>
```

Meta viewport differences

The meta viewport tag is what really makes mobiles … well … mobile! Without it, mobile browsers will assume that it is a desktop site and everything will be small and require pinch-and-zoom:

```
<meta name="viewport" content="width=device-width, initial-scale=1,
maximum-scale=1.0, user-scalable=no">
```

This meta viewport tag is different in that it actually prevents all pinch-and-zoom action. Why? Because, now smart phones are in the hands of more than just the technical elite who know about such things. I've personally seen people accidentally zoom in while just trying to tap a link. They had no idea what they had done or how to get out of it. Regardless, if you use jQuery Mobile, your users have no need of zoom anyway:

```
<linkrel="stylesheet" href="css/custom.css" />
```

We will need custom styles. There's no way around it. Even if we use the jQuery Mobile ThemeRoller (`http://jquerymobile.com/themeroller/`), there's always something that needs overriding. This is where you put it:

```
<script src="js/custom-scripting.js"></script>
```

Originally mentioned under the section regarding global configuration (`http://jquerymobile.com/demos/1.1.0/docs/api/globalconfig.html`), this is where you put your global overrides, as well as any scripts you may want to run or have available universally:

```
<a href="{dynamic location}" class="fullSiteLinmk">View Full Site</a>
```

Most mobile websites follow the "best practice" of including a link to the full site. It's usually in the footer and it usually links to the homepage of the full site. OK, great. The job is done right? Wrong! The best practice would be better labeled as the "industry standard" because there is a better way.

Full-site links beyond the industry standard

The industry standard of simply including a full-site link fails to support the user's mental state. When a user navigates around on the mobile site, they're giving a pretty clear indication of what they want to look at. Supporting the user's mental model as they transition from mobile to full site is more work, but crafting a good user experience always is.

Picture this. Sally is looking around on our mobile site because she wants to buy from us. She has actually taken the time to surf down or search to the product that she wants to see. However, due to the constraints of mobile, we made a few conscious choices to not put all the information there. We only included the high points that market research showed people really cared about. At this point, she might be a little bit frustrated as she taps on the full-site link to try to get more information. The full-site link was coded the traditional (lazy) way and takes her to the root of the full site where she now has to go find the product again. Now she has to do it using pinch-and-zoom, which only adds to the aggravation level. Unless Sally is desperately interested, what what's the chance she'd continue looking on her mobile and what's the chance she'd come back on a desktop browser after such a miserable experience?

Now, instead, picture that same mobile product page having been thoughtfully crafted to point the full-site link at the product page desktop view. This is exactly what we did at my place of employment. Every possible mobile page was explicitly mapped to its desktop equivalent. The seamless transition was taken to user testing with actual customers and was met with a mix of 50 percent ambivalence and 50 percent delight. There was certainly surprise on the users' side because it did violate their expectations, but there was not a single negative reaction. If this does not successfully argue the case for rethinking the way full-site links are traditionally approached, I don't know what does. Preserve the user's mental model. Preserve the contextual relevance.

Naturally, you'll probably have user experience professionals who will use buzzwords like "consistency," "best pracitce," "industry standards," and "violating user expectations." If the evidence from the user tests does not convince them, give them a dose of the following philosophy:

- **Consistency**: This approach is consistent within itself. Every full-site link maps to that page on the full site.

- **Best practices**: A practice is only best until a new practice, comes along that is better. If they would rather keep with *old* best practices then perhaps they should sell their car, and get a horse and buggy.

- **Industry standards**: Industry standards are the crutch upon which the rest of the world tries to hobble along while trying not to fall too far behind the innovators. Good is often the enemy of great. Don't settle for it.

- **Violating user's expectations**: If we tell our users that we're going to send them a free MP3 player and we send them a 128 GB iPad 4, have we violated their expectations? Yep! Think they'll mind? Some expectations are worth violating.

Let's consider the flip side. What if the user really did want to go to the full-site's starting page? Well, they're only one step away because all they have to do now is hit the home button. So, in all likelihood, we will have saved the user several steps of navigation and, at worst, cost them one extra step to get back to the beginning.

It's the little details that take a product from good to great. This is certainly a little detail but I challenge you to spend the extra 30 seconds per page to do this part of the job right.

The global JavaScript

Thanks to the Ajax navigation and progressive enhancement inherent in jQuery Mobile, there are a lot of different and extra events. Let's consider the three unique jQuery Mobile events I've found most useful. We're not going to immediately use them, just be aware of them and be sure to read the comments. Eventually, we'll create `/js/global.js` to house the scripts that we'll need. For now, just read the following script:

```
// JavaScript Document

$('div[data-role="page"]').live( 'pageinit',
function(event){
    /* Triggered on the page being initialized, after
       initialization occurs. We recommend binding to this
       event instead of DOM ready() because this will work
       regardless of whether the page is loaded directly or
       if the content is pulled into another page as part of
       the Ajax navigation system. */
});

$('div[data-role="page"]').live('pagebeforeshow', function(event){
    /* Triggered on the "toPage" we are transitioning to,
       before the actual transition animation is kicked off.
       Callbacks for this event will receive a data object as
       their 2nd arg. This data object has the following
       properties on it: */
});

$('div[data-role="page"]').live( 'pageshow',
function(event){
    /* Triggered on the "toPage" after the transition
       animation has completed. Callbacks for this event will
       receive a data object as their 2nd arg. This data
       object has the following properties on it: */
});
```

.live versus .on

One thing you may have noticed here is that we are using the .live method to capture events. This method has been deprecated since jQuery 1.7. As of the time of this writing, we're on jQuery 1.9. However, even when you look at the examples of event handlers in the documentation, they're still using .live in multiple places.

The .live function works to check every event that bubbled up to the document level and see if it matches the selector. If so, the function is executed. The reason .live was so useful was that it was great at dealing with shifting and dynamically-injected elements. After all, it's hard to bind to something that's not there yet. But you could always count on .live to catch the events. Due to its overused and general inefficiency, it was deprecated in favor of .on. So, here is how we would accomplish the same thing using the following new method:

```
$('div[data-role="page"]').live( 'pageinit', function(event){
  var $page = $(this);
});
```

would become

```
$(document).on('pageinit', function(event){
  var $page = $(event.target);
});
```

This works great if you're looking to address every page. Now let's consider a piece of code that could be used to individually target a single page's initialization:

```
$('#someRandomPage').live( 'pageinit', function(event){
  var $page = $(this);
});
```

would become

```
$(document).on('pageinit', '#someRandomPage', function(event){
  var $page = $(event.target);
});
```

The differences are subtle and, in the end, it's not going to make an ounce of difference from a performance perspective for us because we're dealing with a framework that was designed around letting the page events bubble up to the document level. You will realize no performance boost by using .on versus .live in a jQuery Mobile implementation. However, you may experience an upgrade headache when you are forced to update because they finally did away with .live.

The global CSS

In case this is your first exposure to responsive web design, for the most part, all your custom styles will be in the default section. The other sections are for overriding your default styles to tweak for other device widths and resolutions. The Horizontal Tweaks section is for overriding styles for landscape orientation. The iPad section is geared for tablet resolutions between 768px and 1024px. In the HD and Retina Tweaks section, you will most likely be only overriding background image styles to substitute higher resolution graphics. We'll soon see examples of these in action and we'll put what we use into /css/custom.css. In the mean time, just look at these structures.

```
/* CSS Document */
/* Default Styles     ------------*/



/* Horizontal Tweaks    ----------*/
@media all and (min-width: 480px){

}

/* HD and Retina Tweaks ---------*/
@media only screen and (-webkit-min-device-pixel-ratio: 1.2),
only screen and (min--moz-device-pixel-ratio: 1.2),
only screen and (min-resolution: 240dpi) {

}

/* iPad ----------------*/
@media only screen and (min-device-width: 768px)
and (max-device-width: 1024px) {

}
```

Breaking the HTML into a server side template

Normally, I'm a Java guy, but I've chosen PHP due to the prevalence of the **LAMP (Linux, Apache, MySql, PHP)** platform. All we're really doing here is using variable and Server Side Includes to give our templates consistency and flexibility.

This is not actual production code here. This is just a break down of the initial HTML into a nice PHP boilerplate. If you want to save this to a file for now, may I suggest /boilerplate.php:

```php
<?php
    /* the document title in the <head> */
    $documentTitle = "jQuery Mobile PHP Boilerplate";

    /* Left link of the header bar
     *
     * NOTE: If you set the $headerLeftLinkText = 'Back'
     * then it will become a back button, in which case,
     * no other field for $headerLeft need to be defined.
     */
    $headerLeftHref = "/";
    $headerLeftLinkText = "Home";
    $headerLeftIcon = "home";

    /* The text to show up in the header bar */
    $headerTitle = "Boilerplate";

    /* Right link of the heaer bar */
    $headerRightHref = "tel:8165557438";
    $headerRightLinkText = "Call";
    $headerRightIcon = "grid";

    /* The href to the full-site link */
    $fullSiteLinkHref = "/";
?>
<!DOCTYPE html>
<html>
  <head>
    <?php include "includes/meta.php" ?>
  </head>
  <body>
    <div data-role="page">

      <?php include "includes/header.php" ?>

      <div data-role="content">
        <p>Page Body content</p>
      </div>

      <?php include "includes/footer.php" ?>
    </div>
  </body>
</html>
```

Now we'll extract most of the header and put it into /includes/meta.php:

```
<meta charset="utf-8">
<meta name="viewport" content="width=device-width, initial-scale=1,
maximum-scale=1.0, user-scalable=no">
<linkrel="stylesheet" href="http://code.jquery.com/mobile/1.2.0/
jquery.mobile-1.2.0.min.css" />
<linkrel="stylesheet" href="css/custom.css" />
<scriptsrc="http://code.jquery.com/jquery-1.8.2.min.js"></script>
<!-- from https://raw.github.com/carhartl/jquery-cookie/master/jquery.
cookie.js-->
<scriptsrc="js/jquery.cookie.js"></script>
<scriptsrc="js/global.js"></script>
<scriptsrc="http://code.jquery.com/mobile/1.2.0/jquery.mobile-
1.2.0.min.js"></script>src="http://code.jquery.com/mobile/1.1.0/
jquery.mobile-1.1.0.min.js"></script>


<title><?=$documentTitle?></title>
```

 Note the cookies plugin in js/jquery.cookie.js. You'll want to download this from https://github.com/carhartl/jquery-cookie. We'll use it later in mobile detection.

Now, let's take the page header, make it dynamic, and drop the contents into /includes/header.php:

```
<div data-role="header">
<?PHP if(strtoupper ($headerLeftLinkText) == "BACK"){?> <a data-
icon="arrow-l" href="javascript://"
data-rel="back"><?=$headerLeftLinkText?></a>
<?PHP } else if($headerLeftHref != ""){ ?>
<a<?PHP if($headerLeftIcon != ""){ ?>
data-icon="<?=$headerLeftIcon ?>"
<?PHP } ?>href="<?=$headerLeftHref?>"><?=$headerLeftLinkText?></a>
<?PHP } ?>

<h1><?=$headerTitle ?></h1>

<?PHP if($headerRightHref != ""){ ?>
<a<?PHP if($headerRightIcon != ""){ ?>
data-icon="<?=$headerRightIcon ?>"
data-iconpos="right"
<? } ?>
href="<?=$headerRightHref?>"><?=$headerRightLinkText?></a>
<?PHP } ?>
</div><!-- /header -->
```

Next, let's take the footer content and extract it into `/includes/footer.php`:

```
<div data-role="footer">
<insert 2 spaces>
<h4>Footer content</h4>
</div><!-- /footer -->
<p class="fullSite">
<a class="fullSiteLink" href="<?=$fullSiteLinkHref?>">View Full Site</
a>
</p>
<p class="copyright">&copy; 2012</p>
```

The header and footer PHP files are set-and-forget files. All we have to do is
fill in a few variables on the main page and the `meta.php`, `header.php`, and
`footer.php` will take care of the rest. The `headers.php` is coded such that if your
`$headerLeftLinkText` is set to the word `Back` regardless of casing, it will turn the
left-side button of the header into a back button.

What we need to create our site

We have a viable boilerplate. We have a customer. Let's get to work and code what
we drew in *Chapter 1, Prototyping jQuery Mobile*. For this chapter, we'll stick to just
the first screen since it's all we need to teach the skills.

Here's what we need to think about:

- Logo: We'll simply include the logo from the desktop view.

- Buttons: There are several ways we could accomplish these. At first glance, we might think about using standard `data-role="button"` links. We could leverage a `ui-grid` (`http://jquerymobile.com/demos/1.2.0/docs/content/content-grids.html`) to add the formatting. If we were only intending to optimize for phones held vertically, that would be a great approach. However, we're going to think outside the box here and create a responsive menu that will react well at different resolutions.

- Icons: Those are not standard jQuery Mobile icons. There are countless icon sets online that we could use but let's go with **Glyphish** (`http://glyphish.com/`). They make high-quality icons that include multiple sizes, retina display optimizations, and the original Adobe Illustrator files just in case you want to tweak them. It's an excellent value.

- Customer testimonials: This looks like it would be perfectly suited to a listview with images. We'll pull this content from their Facebook page.

Getting Glyphish and defining custom icons

Glyphish has a license that allows for free use with attribution. The free set (`http://www.glyphish.com/download/`) has only one size and 200 icons, the "Pro" set has multiple sizes, 400 icons, and an unlimited license. For only $25 dollars, that's a no-brainer.

Creating a button with an icon is very simple. All you have to do is use the `data-icon` attribute. Code, such as the following, will yield a button as shown in the following figure:

```
<a href="index.html" data-role="button"
data-icon="delete">Delete</a>
```

What you may not yet realize is the way the jQuery Mobile actually does this. Whatever you have written as the value for `data-icon` will become a class name on the button. If you have an attribute of `data-icon="directions"` then the class that is applied by jQM is `ui-icon-directions`. Naturally, you'll need to craft this in your own custom CSS file like this. We'll put this, and others like it, into `css/custom.css`.

```
.ui-icon-directions{
    background-image:
    url(../icons/icons-gray/113-navigation.png);
    height:28px;
    width:28px;
    background-size:28px 28px;
    margin-left: -14px !important;
}
```

Another thing you'll need to do is get rid of the colored disk around the typical icons. We'll also need to remove the border radius or our icons will get cut off to fit within the shape of the circular radius defined within the style for ui-icon. To do this, we'll add the glyphishIcon class to each link we want to customize this way. We'll also need to add this definition to our custom.css:

```
.glyphishIcon .ui-icon{
    -moz-border-radius: 0px;
    -webkit-border-radius: 0px;
border-radius: 0px;
background-color:transparent;
}
```

In the end, our code for the four buttons on the front page would look as follows:

```
<div class="homeMenu">
  <a class="glyphishIcon" href=" https://maps.google.com/maps?q=9771
+N+Cedar+Ave,+Kansas+City,+MO+64157&hl=en&sll=39.20525,-94.526954&ss
pn=0.014499,0.033002&hnear=9771+N+Cedar+Ave,+Kansas+City,+Missouri
+64157&t=m&z=17&iwloc=A" data-role="button" data-icon="directions"
data-inline="true" data-iconpos="top">Map it</a>
  <a class="glyphishIcon" href="tel:+18167816500" data-role="button"
data-inline="true" data-icon="iphone" data-iconpos="top">Call Us</a>
  <a class="glyphishIcon" href="https://touch.facebook.com/
nickyspizzanickyspizza" data-role="button" data-icon="facebook"
data-iconpos="top" data-inline="true">Like Us</a>
  <a class="glyphishIcon" href="menu.php" data-role="button"
data-inline="true" rel="external" data-icon="utensils" data-
iconpos="top">Menu</a>
</div>
```

It would be rendered on the screen as shown in the following screenshot:

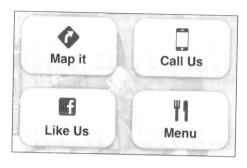

Linking to phones, e-mails, and maps

Mobile browsers have a distinct usability advantage. If we want to link to an e-mail address, the native e-mail client will instantly pop up. The following code is an example:

```
<a href="mailto:shane@roughlybrilliant.com" >email me</a>
```

We can do the same thing with phone numbers and every device will instantly pop up an option to call that number. This is the functionality unmatched on desktops, since most do not have telephony. Here is the href element from the preceding code:

```
href="tel:+18167816500"
```

Maps are another specialty for mobile, since virtually all smart phones have built-in GPS software. Here's the href element for the maps link. It's just a standard link to Google Maps:

```
href="https://maps.google.com/maps?q=9771+N+Cedar+Ave,+Kansas+City,+
MO+64157"
```

For iOS 5 and Android, the OS will intercept that click and bring up the location in the native maps app. Version 6 of iOS changes this model, but we can still link to the Google Maps link and the users will be shown the web view and prompted to open it in Google Maps for iOS, as shown in the following screenshot:

For platforms other than iOS and Android, the user will simply be taken to the Google Maps site. This is good because Google has done an amazing job of making the site usable on any device, including non-smart phones.

Of course, we could leave it at this and call it good enough, but we could do a little more work to give the Apple users a better experience by sending them to the native Apple Maps application. This code will create an object with configurable properties for configuration and future adaptations. It works by version sniffing to see if the major version of the OS is greater than 5. If so, it will assimilate the Google Maps links.

There are two ways these links can be converted. First, it will look for an attribute of `data-appleMapsUrl` on the hyperlink and use it. If that is not present on the link, it will check the `forceAppleMapsConversionIfNoAlt` configuration option to see if you have configured the switcher object to convert the Google Maps link directly.

Once the system realizes that this phone needs switching, it stores that fact into `localStorage` so it won't have to do the work of version checking again. It will simply check the value in `localStorage` for `true`.

Following is the code which is located in the `/js/global.js`:

```
var conditionalAppleMapsSwitcher = {
  appleMapsAltAttribute:"data-appleMapsUrl",
  forceAppleMapsConversionIfNoAlt:true,
  iPhoneAgent:"iPhone OS ",
  iPadAgent:"iPad; CPU OS ",
  process: function(){
    try{
      var agent = navigator.userAgent;
      if(window.localStorage && localStorage.
getItem("replaceWithAppleMaps")){
        if(localStorage.getItem("replaceWithAppleMaps") == "true"){
          this.assimilateMapLinks();
        }
      }else{
        var iOSAgent = null;
        if(agent.indexOf(this.iPhoneAgent) > 0){
          iOSAgent = this.iPhoneAgent
        }
        else if(agent.indexOf(this.iPadAgent) > 0){
          iOSAgent = this.iPadAgent
        }
        if(iOSAgent){
          var endOfAgentStringIndex = (agent.
indexOf(iOSAgent)+iOSAgent.length);
          var version = agent.substr(endOfAgentStringIndex, agent.
indexOf(" " , endOfAgentStringIndex));
          var majorVersion = Number(version.substr(0, version.
indexOf("_")));
          if(majorVersion > 5){
            localStorage.setItem("replaceWithAppleMaps", "true");
            this.assimilateMapLinks();
          }
        }
      }
    }catch(e){}
  },
```

```
assimilateMapLinks:function(){
    try{
        var switcher = this;
        $("a[href^='http://maps.google.com']").each(function(index,
element) {
            var $link = $(element);
            if($link.attr(switcher.appleMapsAltAttribute)){
                $link.attr("href", $link.attr(switcher.
appleMapsAltAttribute));
            }else if(switcher.forceAppleMapsConversionIfNoAlt){
                $link.attr("href", $link.attr("href").replace(/maps\.
google\.com\/maps/,"maps.apple.com/"));
            }
        });
    }catch(e){}
}
```

}With this code, it is now very easy to simply call it on `pageinit` from our `/js/global.js`:

```
$(document).on("pageinit", function(){
    conditionalAppleMapsSwitcher.process();
});
```

This approach is completely seamless to the user. No matter what system they are on, they will have the most frictionless experience in trying to reach your client's business.

Custom fonts

Custom fonts are present on their full site (and, thus, part of their branding). These fonts will work just as well on mobile. Platforms like iOS, Android, and the latest Blackberry fully support `@font-face` CSS. Older editions of BlackBerry and Windows Phone may or may not support `@font-face` depending on the model that users have. For anyone that does not support `@font-face`, they will simply be presented with standard web fonts as you specify in the `font-family` rule. There are many different web font providers:

- **Google Web Fonts** (`http://www.google.com/webfonts/`)
- **TypeKit** (`https://typekit.com/`)
- **Font Squirrel** (`http://www.fontsquirrel.com/`)
- **Fonts.com Web Fonts** (`http://www.fonts.com/web-fonts`)

For our project we're going to use Google Web Fonts. We'll need to include these lines in the <head> of every page that we want to use them. Since we'll probably be using them everywhere, let's just include these lines in our file /includes/meta.php.

```
<link href='http://fonts.googleapis.com/css?family=Marvel'
rel='stylesheet' type='text/css'>
```

Once we have linked our fonts in the <head>, we'll need to specify their usage in a font-family rule within our /css/custom.css file as follows:

```
h1,h2,h3,.cardo{font-family: Marvel, sans-serif;}
```

Now, for any browser (which is most these days) that supports it, they'll see something as follows:

What customers are saying:

 A word of caution: Web fonts are not exactly lightweight. Marvel weighs in at 20 KB. Not huge, but not small. You would not want to include too many of these.

Page curl shadow effects for our list items

We'll be laying out the customer testimonials in unordered lists. We could use an image listview, but we want some spacing in between each item as well as a page curl effect. So, let's just style a regular unordered list. Whenever possible, we should avoid overriding the standard jQuery Mobile code. It's just asking for trouble. Whenever you override something that is built to be a framework (like jQuery Mobile), you run the risk of the next release completely breaking the overrides and custom adaptations you have made.

The code for this customization will be displayed and labeled in the final CSS a little later in this chapter. The point is, we're going to do this using CSS3. Most mobile browsers fully support CSS3, including transformations, transitions, animations, shadows, gradients, and rounded corners. Ancient platforms, such as Windows Phone 7 and BlackBerry 5 are based on Internet Explorer 7 or earlier and do not fully support CSS3. In those cases, rather than seeing the fancy page curl, they'll just see a white box containing and image and text. While not ideal, it's a perfectly reasonable fallback.

Optimization: why you should be thinking of it first

I believe that optimization is important enough that you need to know and be aware of it at the beginning. You are going to do some awesome work and I don't want you or your stakeholders to think it's any less awesome, or slow, or anything else because you didn't know the tricks to squeeze the most performance out of your systems. It's never too early to impress people with the performance of your creations. Mobile is a very unforgiving environment and some of the tips in this section will make more difference than any of the "best coding practices."

From a performance perspective, there is absolutely nothing worse than an HTTP request. That's why CSS sprites are a good idea. Every request we make slows us down because the TCP/IP protocol assumes that each request's available bandwidth starts at near zero. So, not only do we have the communication's lag time to start pulling assets from the server, it also takes a ramp up time before that asset is transmitted at full possible speed. 4G isn't going, to save us from these facts. Sure, their transfer rates are great once they get going but the lag time it takes to actually begin the process of transfer is what kills us. We also have to consider how often users find themselves with few or no bars of reception. This is especially true in buildings. So, here are some tips for optimizing your mobile site:

- **Reduce HTTP requests by combining as many assets as possible.** When the **SPDY protocol** (`http://www.chromium.org/spdy/spdy-whitepaper/`) finally gains traction, it will solve our problems, but, for now and the foreseeable future, this is what slows us down the most. This is also why I will not be advising the user on tools like **Require.js** (`http://requirejs.org/`) to dynamically load in whatever is necessary for that page in chunks. Don't be lazy. Know what your page needs and combine as much as possible.

- **Turn on gzip compression on your server.** There's a pretty good chance that any given server has gzip compression enabled but you should check. This will shrink your text-based assets (HTML, CSS, JS) by up to 70 percent for transmission. It actually makes more of a difference than minifying your code. For more on this, check out `https://developers.google.com/speed/articles/gzip`.

- **Minify.** Minifying is the process by which a perfectly human-readable piece of code is stripped of all the useful whitespace, formatting, and comments. All that is pushed to the browser is the code. Some go so far as to actually change the variable and function names into one or two letter substitutions. This is really only a good idea for longstanding, highly-stable code. Libraries, such as jQuery, that have a tendency to be large in the first place will definitely benefit. However, for your own code, it's a good idea to leave it human-readable so you can debug things if you have to. Just try to keep your HTML pages under 25 KB (uncompressed) and your JS and CSS files under 1 MB (also uncompressed). A study conducted by Yahoo shows that across all platforms, this seems to be the lowest common denominator that devices will allow to be cached between visits (`http://www.yuiblog.com/blog/2010/07/12/mobile-browser-cache-limits-revisited/`).

- **Caching and Microcaching**. If you're on Apache like most of the rest of the web (`http://news.netcraft.com/archives/2012/01/03/january-2012-web-server-survey.html`), you can easily setup caching using an `htaccess` file. If you specify a caching time of one month for a type of asset, then browsers will attempt to hold those assets in cache for one month without even checking to see if there is anything new on the server. Be careful here. You don't want to set long cache times for anything you might want to be able to change quickly. However, things like JavaScript libraries and images that don't change can certainly be cached without any ill effects.

  In order to protect yourself from traffic flooding, you can use the `htaccess` caching rules to make pages last for something as small as a minute using code such as the following:

  ```
  # 1 MIN
  <filesMatch "\.(html|htm|php)$">
    Header set Cache-Control "max-age=60, private, proxy-revalidate"
  </filesMatch>
  ```

  You can learn more on caching with htaccess at `http://www.askapache.com/htaccess/speed-up-sites-with-htaccess-caching.html`.

- **Do NOT use images if it can be done in CSS3.** The CSS3 standard started back in 1999. The W3C started working on its first draft for the CSS4 recommendation back in 2009. It's time to move the web forward and leave legacy browsers to the ash heap of history. If someone is using a browser that doesn't support CSS gradients, let them default back to the solid background color they so richly deserve. If their browser doesn't support rounded corners in CSS, then they'll just have to make do with square corners.

If a potential client wants you to go beyond the web standards to support ancient technologies or insists on pixel-perfect designs, fire the client or charge them enough extra to make it worth your time. Pixel-perfect designs are hard enough on desktops. Mobile is the Wild, Wild West where everybody is implementing their solutions just differently enough that you'll never achieve pixel-perfect solutions. (http://dowebsitesneedtolookexactlythesameineverybrowser.com/)

Use CSS3 in lieu of images when possible to save on weight and HTTP requests. Most modern smart phones support it now (iOS, Android, BlackBerry 6+, Windows Phone 8+). By 2013 and 2014, virtually all early smart phones will be replaced.

The final product

We now have all the requirements, knowledge, and assets to make the first page. We'll place this code as the first page by naming it index.php. All images are provided in the source folders for the example.

Following is the final code for index.php:

```php
<?php
$documentTitle = "Nicky's Pizza";

$headerLeftHref = "/";
$headerLeftLinkText = "Home";
$headerLeftIcon = "home";

$headerTitle = "Boilerplate";

$headerRightHref = "tel:8165077438";
$headerRightLinkText = "Call";
$headerRightIcon = "grid";

$fullSiteLinkHref = "/";

?>
<!DOCTYPE html>
<html>
<head>
 <?php include("includes/meta.php"); ?>
</head>

<body>
<div data-role="page">
    <div data-role="content">
```

```
      <div class="logoContainer"><img src="images/LogoMobile.png"
alt="Logo" width="290" style="margin:0" /></div>

        <div class="homeMenu">
            <a class="glyphishIcon" href="http://maps.google.com/
maps?q=9771+N+Cedar+Ave,+Kansas+City,+MO+64157&hl=en&sll=39.20525,-
94.526954&sspn=0.014499,0.033002&hnear=9771+N+Cedar+Ave,+Kansas+
City,+Missouri+64157&t=m&z=17&iwloc=A" data-role="button" data-
icon="directions" data-inline="true" data-iconpos="top">Map it</a>
            <a class="glyphishIcon" href="tel:+18167816500"
data-role="button" data-inline="true" data-icon="iphone" data-
iconpos="top">Call Us</a>
            <a class="glyphishIcon" href="https://touch.facebook.com/
nickyspizzanickyspizza" data-role="button" data-icon="facebook" data-
iconpos="top" data-inline="true">Like Us</a>
            <a class="glyphishIcon" href="menu.php" data-role="button"
data-inline="true" rel="external" data-icon="utensils" data-
iconpos="top">Menu</a>
        </div>

        <h3>What customers are saying:</h3>
        <div class="testimonials">
            <ul class="curl">
                <li><img class="facebook" src="images/fb2.jpg"
alt="facebook photo" width="60" height="60" align="left" />I recommend
the Italian Sausage Sandwich. Awesome!! Will be back soon!</li>
                <li><img class="facebook" src="images/fb0.jpg"
alt="facebook photo" width="60" height="60" align="left" />LOVED
your veggie pizza friday night and the kids devoured the cheese with
jalapenos!!! salad was fresh and yummy with your house dressing!!</li>
                <li><img class="facebook" src="images/fb1.jpg"
alt="facebook photo" width="60" height="60" align="left" />The Clarkes
love Nicky's pizza! So happy you are here in liberty.</li>
            </ul>
        </div>

    </div>

    <?php include("includes/footer.php"); ?>
</div>

</body>
</html>
```

The custom CSS

This code from `/css/custom.css` houses everything we've done to customize our look and feel. It includes the definitions for the custom icons, page curls, and custom fonts. Any images referenced were provided by the client and are provided in the final source.

Pay particular attention to the comments here as I have spelled out each section's purpose and how it plays into a *responsive web design*:

```css
@charset "UTF-8";

/**********************************************/
/* define the places we'll use custom fonts */
/**********************************************/

h1,h2,h3,.cardo{font-family: Marvel, sans-serif;}
.logoContainer{
    font-family: Marvel, sans-serif;
    text-align:center;margin:auto;
}
.makersMark{
    margin:1.5em auto;
    font-family: Marvel, sans-serif;
    text-align:center;
}
.testimonials{margin:0 auto;}

/**********************************************/
/*  define the background for the site */
/**********************************************/

.ui-content{
    background-image:url(../images/cropfade.jpg);
    background-repeat:no-repeat;
    background-size: 100%;
}

/**************************************************/
/*  override the listview descriptions to allow them */
/*  to wrap instead of simply cutting off with an */
/*  ellipsis */
/**************************************************/

.ui-li-desc{white-space:normal;}

/**************************************************/
/*  define our custom menu on the front page  */
/**************************************************/

.homeMenu{ text-align:center;}
.homeMenu .ui-btn{ min-width:120px;  margin:.5em;}
.glyphishIcon .ui-icon{
    -moz-border-radius: 0px;
```

```
        -webkit-border-radius: 0px;
        border-radius: 0px;
        background-color:transparent;
    }
    /**********************************************/
    /* define custom icons for our four menu buttons  */
    /**********************************************/

    .ui-icon-directions{
        background-image: url(../icons/icons-gray/113-navigation.png);
        height:28px;
        width:28px;
        background-size:28px 28px;
        margin-left: -14px !important;
      }
    .ui-icon-iphone{
        background-image: url(../icons/icons-gray/32-iphone.png);
        height:28px;
        width:16px;
        background-size:16px 28px;
        margin-left: -8px !important;
      }
    .ui-icon-facebook{
        background-image: url(../icons/icons-gray/208-facebook.png);
        height:28px;
        width:22px;
        background-size:22px 22px;
        margin-left: -11px !important;
    }
    .ui-icon-utensils{
        background-image: url(../icons/icons-gray/48-fork-and-knife.png);
        height:28px;
        width:18px;
        background-size:18px 26px;
        margin-left: -9px !important;
    }


    /**********************************************/
    /* define how to show people's Facebook images
    /**********************************************/

    li img.facebook{padding:0 10px 10px 0;}

    /**********************************************/
    /* define the look of the footer content */
    /**********************************************/
    .fullSite{text-align:center;}
```

```
.copyright{
    text-align:center;font-family: Marvel, sans-serif;
    marign-top:2em;
}


/**********************************************/
/* define how the layout and images will change for */
/* phones in landscape mode.  RESPONSIVE WEB DESGIN */
/**********************************************/

/* Horizontal ----------*/
@media all and (min-width: 480px){

  /**********************************************/
  /* reflow the main menu buttons to display as */
  /* four in a row and give some appropriate margin */
  /**********************************************/
.homeMenu .ui-btn{ min-width:100px;   margin:.2em;}
}


/**********************************************/
/* define how we'll override the image URLs for */
/* devices with high resolutions. */
/* RESPONSIVE WEB DESIGN */
/**********************************************/
@media only screen and (-webkit-min-device-pixel-ratio: 1.5),
only screen and (min--moz-device-pixel-ratio: 1.5),
only screen and (min-resolution: 240dpi) {
.ui-icon-directions{
    background-image: url(../icons/icons-gray/113-navigation@2x.png);
  }
.ui-icon-iphone{
    background-image: url(../icons/icons-gray/32-iphone@2x.png);
  }
.ui-icon-facebook{
    background-image: url(../icons/icons-gray/208-facebook@2x.png);
  }
.ui-icon-utensils{
    background-image: url(../icons/icons-gray/48-fork-and-knife@2x.png);
  }
}

/**********************************************/
/* define the reflow, sizes, spacing for the menu */
/* buttons for iPad.  RESPONSIVE WEB DESIGN
```

```
/***********************************************/
/* iPad size -----------*/
@media only screen and (min-device-width: 768px)
and (max-device-width: 1024px) {
    .homeMenu .ui-btn{ min-width:120px;  margin:.7em; }
}


/***********************************************/
/* begin page curl CSS */
/***********************************************/
ul.curl {
    position: relative;
    z-index: 1;
    list-style: none;
    margin: 0;
    padding: 0;
  }
ul.curl li {
    position: relative;
    float: left;
    padding: 10px;
    border: 1px solid #efefef;
    margin: 10px 0;
    background: #fff;
    -webkit-box-shadow: 0 1px 4px rgba(0, 0, 0, 0.27), 0 0 40px
    rgba(0, 0, 0, 0.06) inset;
    -moz-box-shadow: 0 1px 4px rgba(0, 0, 0, 0.27), 0 0 40px rgba
    (0, 0, 0, 0.06) inset;
    box-shadow: 0 1px 4px rgba(0, 0, 0, 0.27), 0 0 40px rgba
    (0, 0, 0, 0.06) inset;    text-align:left;
}
ul.curlli:before,
ul.curlli:after {
    content: '';
    z-index: -1;
    position: absolute;
    left: 10px;
    bottom: 10px;
    width: 70%;
    max-width: 300px;
    max-height: 100px;
    height: 55%;
    -webkit-box-shadow: 0 8px 16px rgba(0, 0, 0, 0.3);
```

```
    -moz-box-shadow: 0 8px 16px rgba(0, 0, 0, 0.3);
    box-shadow: 0 8px 16px rgba(0, 0, 0, 0.3);
    -webkit-transform: skew(-15deg) rotate(-6deg);
    -moz-transform: skew(-15deg) rotate(-6deg);
    -ms-transform: skew(-15deg) rotate(-6deg);
    -o-transform: skew(-15deg) rotate(-6deg);
    transform: skew(-15deg) rotate(-6deg);
}
ul.curlli:after {
    left: auto;
    right: 10px;
    -webkit-transform: skew(15deg) rotate(6deg);
    -moz-transform: skew(15deg) rotate(6deg);
    -ms-transform: skew(15deg) rotate(6deg);
    -o-transform: skew(15deg) rotate(6deg);
    transform: skew(15deg) rotate(6deg); }
/***********************************************/
/* end page curl CSS */
/***********************************************/
```

The resulting first page

Let's have a look at the final product of our work. On the left-side we have the rendered page in portrait view, and on the right we have the landscape view:

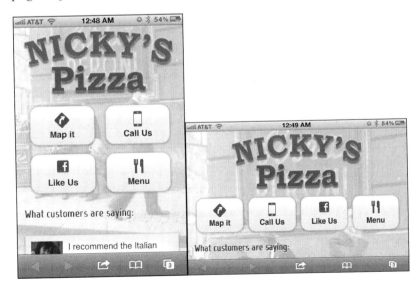

It is important to test your designs in both orientations. It can be rather embarrassing when someone comes along later and breaks your work by doing nothing more than turning their phone.

Here is how it looks on the iPad. There is some matter of debate in the industry as to whether or not the iPad counts as mobile since it has enough resolution and a large enough screen to view normal desktop sites, especially if viewed in landscape mode. People who advocate the desktop view are forgetting a very important fact. The iPad and all the other tablets, such as Kindle Fire, Nook Color, and Google Nexus devices, are still touch interfaces. While full sites are still perfectly readable, interaction points may still be tiny targets. If it's a touch interface, your customer will be better served by jQuery Mobile.

Getting the user to our mobile site

Now that we've got this great start to a mobile site, how does the user get there? `yourdomain.mobi`? `m.yourdomain.com`? The truth is, users don't go to mobile sites. They typically do one of two things: Google the site, or enter in the primary domain into the address bar, the same behavior they use on desktop sites. So, it falls on us to properly detect a mobile user and give them the appropriate interface.

There is much debate in the industry as to how this should be done. Most experts seem to agree that you do not want to get into the business of detecting specific platforms, a practice known as user agent sniffing. At first, it doesn't seem such a bad idea. After all, there's really only the four major platforms: iOS, Android, Windows Phone, and BlackBerry. Even still, this approach can quickly become a nightmare as new platforms are developed in the future or come into dominance. Here's the real question, why would we care what platform they're on? What we really care about is device capability.

Detecting and redirecting using JavaScript

Naturally, this is not going to hit everyone in the mobile market. Even in the United States, the smart phone penetration rate is only 50 percent. (`http://blog.nielsen.com/nielsenwire/online_mobile/smartphones-account-for-half-of-all-mobile-phones-dominate-new-phone-purchases-in-the-us/`) But does it matter? .

If this approach only reaches 50 percent of the market at best, is it truly an appropriate solution? Yes, but how can this be? The following two reasons explain it best:

- People who do not have a smart phone don't usually have a data plan. Surfing the web becomes financially prohibitive. Most people without smart phones and data plans won't be reaching you.
- People who have old smart phones like BlackBerry 5 or earlier may have a data plan. However, those devices have browsers that are barely worth the name and their users know it. They *might* hit your site but it's not likely, and their existence is dropping quickly.

For the most part, anyone who likely would hit your site with a smart phone will respond perfectly. The exceptions are not worth mentioning.

If the device supports media queries and has a touch interface then it's well suited for our mobile site. The only exception to this rule is, of course, Internet Explorer on Windows Phone 7. So, we'll make a slight concession for them. First, we'll need to download the cookie plugin for jQuery. If you haven't yet, get it from `https://github.com/carhartl/jquery-cookie` and put it in the `/js/` folder. This code will be placed on any folder that you want to do mobile redirection.

```
<script type="text/javascript">
  //First, we check the cookies to see if the user has
  //clicked on the full site link.  If so, we don't want
  //to send them to mobile again.  After that, we check for
  //capabilities or if it's IE Mobile
```

```
if("true" != $.cookie("fullSiteClicked") &&
    ('querySelector' in document &&
     'localStorage' in window&&
'addEventListener' in window &&
('ontouchstart' in window ||
window.DocumentTouch && document
instanceOf DocumentTouch
)
)
|| navigator.userAgent.indexOf('IEMobile') > 0
)
{
location.replace(YOUR MOBILE URL);
}
</script>
```

We can also customize the mobile destination on a per-page basis. Pairing this technique with the dynamic full-site link we created earlier will result in a seamless transition between the mobile and desktop view whenever a user wants to switch. We just have one problem now. We need to set a cookie so that, if they tap the full-site link, they won't be pushed right back into mobile. Let's put this into /js/ global.js:

```
$("[data-role='page']").live('pageinit', function (event, ui) {
    $("a.fullSiteLink").click(function(){
    $.cookie("fullSiteClicked","true", {path: "/", expires: 3600});
    });
});
```

It's a good idea to set an expiration on any cookie that you write for mobile devices. On desktops PCs, people tend to close their browsers. On mobile, people click the home button which may or may not actually close that browser's session. On Android, the browser never gets shutdown unless the user does so explicitly.

Detecting on the server

If you simply must get all mobile people to your mobile site, you'll need to do detection on the server using a tool like **WURFL** (`http://wurfl.sourceforge.net/`). It is the ultimate community-maintained database of wireless device descriptors. Essentially, this is user agent sniffing but the database is well maintained by the community. The tool wi ll be able to tell you all kinds of useful things about each device that visits you. The link `http://www.scientiamobile.com/wurflCapability/tree` will give you a complete listing of WURFL's capabilities. We'll get into the nuts and bolts of this in a later chapter.

Summary

We covered a lot of ground in this chapter and we now have all the skills and tools to take what would have been a pretty generic-looking mobile site and turned it into something unique. We know how to make it look unique, how to host it, how to get the user there, and how to give them a more functional parachute if they're unhappy. Already, we're several steps ahead of the average developer who's just getting started and this is only the second chapter. In the next chapter, we'll start looking into more in-depth topics that bigger businesses usually care about, such as validation, analytics, and many more.

3
Analytics, long forms, and frontend validation

Time for growth. Business is picking up and nothing says big business like massive forms, metrics, and customized experiences.

In this chapter, we will cover:

- Google Static Maps
- Google Analytics
- Long and multi-page forms
- Integrating jQuery Validate

Google Static Maps

In the last chapter, we completely geeked out on how to dynamically link directly into the native GPS systems of iOS and Android. Now, let's consider another approach. The client wanted the opportunity to show the user the street address, a map, and give them another chance to call for delivery. In this case, simply linking to the native GPS systems won't suffice. We can still trigger that if the user clicks on the address or the map, but as a step in between, we can inject a static map from Google (`https://developers.google.com/maps/documentation/staticmaps/`).

Is it as whiz-bang as bringing up the app directly to start the turn-by-turn directions? Nope, but it's a heck of a lot faster and may be all that the user needs. They may instantly recognize the location and decide that, yes actually, they would rather call instead. Remember to always approach things from the user's perspective. It's not always about doing the coolest thing we can.

Let's take a look at the drawing that was approved by the client:

Let's look at the code for this page which we'll put into /map.php:

```php
<?php
    $documentTitle = "Map | Nicky's Pizza";

    $fullSiteLinkHref = "/";

    $mapsAddress = "https://maps.google.com/maps?q=9771+N+Cedar+A
ve,+Kansas+City,+MO+64157&hl=en&sll=39.20525,-94.526954&sspn=0
.014499,0.033002&hnear=9771+N+Cedar+Ave,+Kansas+City,+Missouri-
+64157&t=m&z=17&iwloc=A";
    $staticMapUrl = "https://maps.googleapis.com/maps/api/
staticmap?center=39.269109,-94.45281&amp;zoom=15&amp;size=
288x200&amp;markers=color:0xd64044%7Clabel:N%7C39.269109,-
94.45281&amp;sensor=true;"
?>
<!DOCTYPE html>
<html>
<head>
    <?php include("includes/meta.php"); ?>
</head>

<body>
```

```
<div data-role="page">
  <div data-role="content">
    <div class="logoContainer"><img src="images/LogoMobile.png"
alt="Logo" width="290" style="margin:0" /></div>
    <p>
      <a href="<?=$mapsAddress ?>">
        <address class="vcard">
          <div class="adr">
            <div class="street-address">9771 N Cedar Ave</div>
            <span class="locality">Kansas City</span>,
            <span class="region">MO</span>,
            <span class="postal-code">64157</span>
            <div class="country-name">U.S.A.</div>
          </div>
        </address>
      </a>
    </p>
    <p><a href="<?= $mapsAddress ?>"><img src="<?=$staticMapUrl ?>"
width="288" height="200" /></a></p>
    <p><a href="tel:+18167816500" data-role="button">Call for
delivery</a></p>
  </div>
  <?php include("includes/footer.php"); ?>
</div>
</body>
</html>
```

Take note of the use of the microformat (http://microformats.org/) used to mark up the address. This is not necessary but it is pretty standard since 2007, and it's a good way to give your information a little more semantic value. That means that not only can people read it, but even computers can read it and make sense of it. If you'd like to learn more about microformats, you can read this article from Smashing Magazine: http://coding.smashingmagazine.com/2007/05/04/microformats-what-they-are-and-how-to-use-them/

Adding Google Analytics

Every website should have analytics. If not, it's difficult to say how many people are hitting your site, if we're getting people through our conversion funnels, or what pages are causing people to leave our site.

Let's enhance the global JavaScript (/js/global.js) file to automatically log each page as it is shown. This is a very important distinction. In the desktop world, every analytics hit is based on the document ready event. That will not work for **jQuery Mobile (jQM)** because the first page in an Ajax based navigation system is the only one that ever triggers a page load event. In jQM, we need to trigger this on the pageshow event using the following code:

```
/**********************************************/
/* Declare the analytics variables as global */
/**********************************************/
var _gaq = _gaq || [];


/**********************************************/
/* Initialize tracking when the page is loaded*/
/**********************************************/
$(document).ready(function(e) {
(function() {
var ga = document.createElement('script');
ga.type = 'text/javascript';

//Call in the Google Analytics scripts asynchronously.
ga.async = true;
ga.src = ('https:' == document.location.protocol ?
'https://ssl' :
'http://www')
+'.google-analytics.com/ga.js';
var s = document.getElementsByTagName('script')[0];
s.parentNode.insertBefore(ga, s); })();
});


/**********************************************/
/* On every pageshow, register each page view in GA */
/**********************************************/
$("[data-role='page']").live('pageshow', function (event, ui)
{

//wrap 3rd party code you don't control in try/catch
try {
_gaq.push(['_setAccount', 'YOUR ANALYTICS ID']);
if ($.mobile.activePage.attr("data-url")) {
_gaq.push(['_trackPageview',
```

```
//Pull the page to track from the data-url attribute
//of the active page.
$.mobile.activePage.attr("data-url")]);
} else {
_gaq.push(['_trackPageview']);
}
}
   //if there is an error, let's dump it to the console
catch(err) {console.log(err);}
});
```

By using an asynchronous call to pull in Google Analytics, we are allowing the user to proceed, even if tracking is non-functional or taking a while to load. Typically, a call to a JavaScript file will pause all further asset loading and JavaScript execution until the requested script has been fully loaded and executed. We really don't want to have our otherwise well-crafted, speedy, and functioning page held up because some ad network or analytics tracking is taking a while to respond.

We pull the location to be tracked from the data-url attribute of the current page because you cannot reliably use the document.location function for your page hit tracking. jQM's Ajax based navigation leads to some very strange URLs in your tracking. The jQM team is working on that but it will be a while until the needed technology is present on all devices. Instead, just pull the URL to track from the data-url attribute of the jQM page. If you dynamically create your pages, this is where you would also put the custom name for your page for tracking purposes. If you're using multi-page templates, each page's ID will be tracked as the page view.

We really haven't done much analytics work yet, but let's look at some of the insights we can already start to glean. Here is just a sample of the technology breakdowns:

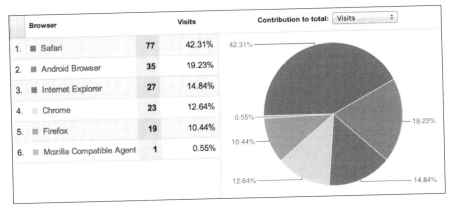

The following image shows a full report of the same view broken down a little further to show which devices are most poplar:

		Mobile Device Info	Operating System	Visits ↓	Pages / Visit	Avg. Visit Duration	% New Visits	Bounce Rate
☐	1.	Apple iPhone	iOS	41	7.05	00:06:12	58.54%	12.20%
☐	2.	Apple iPad	iOS	19	8.95	00:02:50	68.42%	21.05%
☐	3.	(not set)	Android	10	4.70	00:02:47	20.00%	20.00%
☐	4.	SonyEricsson LT15i Xperia Arc	Android	8	6.88	00:03:20	50.00%	12.50%
☐	5.	HTC EVO 4G	Android	4	2.25	00:01:09	50.00%	50.00%
☐	6.	RIM BlackBerry 9800 Torch	BlackBerry	4	10.00	00:07:10	25.00%	25.00%
☐	7.	Samsung SPH-D700 Epic 4G	Android	4	13.50	00:04:56	75.00%	0.00%
☐	8.	Fujitsu Toshiba T-01C REGZA Phone T-01C	Android	2	24.50	00:14:10	100.00%	0.00%
☐	9.	Samsung SPH-D710	Android	2	4.00	00:00:39	50.00%	50.00%
☐	10.	(not set)	Windows Phone	1	3.00	00:01:02	100.00%	0.00%

Pay attention to the **Bounce Rate** column in the previous image on each platform as a whole. If one is significantly higher than the other, it could be an indicator that we need to look a little closer at our site on that device.

	Page	Pageviews	% Pageviews
1.	/m/menu.php	290	26.10%
2.	/m/	210	18.90%
3.	/menu.html	110	9.90%
4.	/	107	9.63%
5.	/specialty_pizza	66	5.94%
6.	/index.html	58	5.22%
7.	/custom_pizza	52	4.68%
8.	/m/map.php	49	4.41%
9.	/history.html	35	3.15%
10.	/appetizers	30	2.70%

Making a mobile website is about much more than simply making it look pretty on mobile browsers. The best indicator of a well-tailored mobile site is that people are able to get in and find what they need quickly. That makes the Top Content report our new best friend.

Unsurprisingly, most people who come to the site are hitting the menu as shown in the report in the previous image. However, the menu is nothing but a starting point. What are they most interested in within the menu? Specialty pizzas. It is this kind of an insight that can lead you to a successful first redesign. Perhaps, we should think about featuring the specialties on the homepage and save our users time.

The bottom line is, without good analytics, you have no idea if you're building the right thing. The site, as designed right now, is making them go two clicks deep to see what's most cared about, or is it?

So far, we've only tracked page views. But, in the mobile word, that's not the whole picture. What about the links that dial the phone number but do not fire a page view? What about links that go off-site to Facebook or to mapping software, such as Google Maps? Those certainly count as further interactions but it would be nice to have numbers on all of these kinds of clicks too. We're already tracking page views differently, let's continue.

Naturally, we want to track custom events and not have to write JavaScript for every event we want to track. Let's make our links like this:

```
<a href="tel:+18167816500" data-pageview="call">Call Us</a>
```

Then, let's add a little more to the `pageinit` handler using the following code:

```
$(document).on('pageinit', function (event, ui) {
$page = $(event.target);

$page.find("[data-pageview]").click(function(){
var $eventTarget = $(this);
if($eventTarget.attr("data-pageview") == "href"){
_gaq.push(['_trackPageview',
$eventTarget.attr("href")]);
}else{
_gaq.push(['_trackPageview',
$eventTarget.attr("data-pageview")]);
}
});
```

There is a lot more that can be done with analytics tracking such as custom event tracking, e-commerce campaign tracking, goals tracking, and so on. Now that you know the basics of how to tie Google Analytics into jQuery Mobile, you can continue to explore more tracking as wisdom dictates by looking here: `https://developers.google.com/analytics/devguides/collection/gajs/`.

Long and multi-page forms

On desktops, long forms are pretty normal. We've all seen registration pages and e-commerce ordering processes. The longer the form is, the greater the tendency to try to break them up into smaller, more logical pieces. This is usually done in a couple of ways:

- Leave it as a full page but inject enough whitespace and grouping that it doesn't look quite so intimidating

- Either physically break the form into multiple pages or use show/hide techniques to accomplish the same thing

Neither of these approaches makes a lot of difference with regards to task completion. Either way, both methods are particularly unfavorable strategies within the constraints of mobile. The best things we can do to increase success are:

- Completely eliminate all optional fields

- Reduce the number of required fields as much as possible (get vicious about it)

- Pre-fill elements with reasonable defaults

- Validate fields immediately instead of waiting till the end

- Give the user upfront notice about how long the task is likely to take

Even doing this, sometimes forms are just going to be long. If you run into this situation, here is a useful way of taking a long form and breaking it into several pages using jQuery Mobile. Here is the code from `ordercheckout.php`:

```
<body>
 <form action="/m/processOrder.php" method="post">
  <div data-role="page" id="delivery">
    <?php $headerTitle = "Deliver To"; ?>
    <?php include("includes/header.php"); ?>
    <div data-role="content">
    <h2>Where will we be delivering?</h2>

      <!--form elements go here -->

    <p>
      <div class="ui-grid-a">
```

```
            <div class="ui-block-a"><a data-role="button" href="index.
php">Cancel</a></div>
            <div class="ui-block-b"><a data-role="button"
href="#payment">Continue</a></div>
          </div>
        </p>

    </div>
    <?php include("includes/footer.php"); ?>
  </div>

  <div data-role="page" id="payment">
    <?php $headerTitle = "Payment"; ?>
    <?php include("includes/header.php"); ?>
    <div data-role="content">
      <h2>Please enter payment information</h2>

        <!--form elements go here -->

      <p>
        <div class="ui-grid-a">
          <div class="ui-block-a"><a data-role="button" data-theme="d"
href="index.php">Cancel</a></div>
          <div class="ui-block-b"><input type="submit"data-theme="b"
value="Submit"/></div>
          </div>
        </p>

    </div>
      <?php include("includes/footer.php"); ?>
  </div>

  </form>
  <body>
```

The very first thing to note here is that the body and form tags are outside all jQuery Mobile pages. Remember, all of this is just one big Data Object Model (DOM). All the crazy progressive enhancements and page shifting in the UI don't change that. This page, at its heart, is one massive form that we will use to submit the entire order process all at once.

Integrating jQuery Validate

It's always been important to the user experience to validate as much as possible on the client. HTML5 goes a long way to this end by giving far greater control over input types. As good as HTML5 input types are, we'll need more. Enter Query Validate. (`http://bassistance.de/jquery-plugins/jquery-plugin-validation/`)

The Validate plugin is a staple in the jQuery community but there are certain things that will help our mobile implementation. Let's start with automatically adding validation to any page that has a form with a class of `validateMe`.

```
$("form.validateMe").each(function(index, element) {
var $form = $(this);
var v = $form.validate({
errorPlacement: function(error, element) {
vardataErrorAt = element.attr("data-error-at");
    if (dataErrorAt)
        $(dataErrorAt).html(error);
    else
      error.insertBefore(element);
    }
  });
});
```

Since it is possible that a page might contain multiple forms, let's just deal with it now by hooking it into every form that requests validation, using the following command:

```
$("form.validateMe").each
```

By default, `ValidateMe` places errors after the invalid field. That won't do in mobile because the errors would show up underneath the form element. On BlackBerry and some Android systems, the form element is not necessarily centered vertically within the space between the keyboard and the field itself. If the user has botched it, the feedback won't be immediate and obvious. That's why we are making two changes to the error placement using the following code line:

```
errorPlacement:
```

On any given element, we can specify where we want the error to be placed using standard jQuery selectors, as shown in the following code line. Perhaps we'll never use it but it's handy to have.

```
element.attr("data-error-at");
```

If no error placement has been specified at the element level, we'll inset the error before the element itself, as shown in the following code line. Error language will show up between the label text and the form element. This way, the keyboard will never eclipse the feedback.

```
error.insertBefore(element);
```

In a single-form, multi-page environment, we want to be able to validate one jQM page at a time before proceeding to the next page. The first thing we'll need to do is give an alternate way of dealing with the `required` function, since we're clearly not validating the entire form at once.

This can be declared outside any functions in our global script:

```
$.validator.addMethod("pageRequired", function(value, element) {
var $element = $(element);
   if ($element.closest("."+$.mobile.subPageUrlKey).hasClass($.mobile.
activePageClass)){
      return !this.optional(element);
}
   return "dependency-mismatch";
}, $.validator.messages.required);
```

Adding additional `validator` methods like this are very handy. We can declare our own validation methods for just about anything.

For your quick reference, here are the other Validate options:

- required
- remote
- email
- url
- date
- dateISO
- number
- digits
- creditcard
- equalTo
- accept
- maxlength
- minlength
- rangelength

- range

- max

- min

For more inspiring demos, please check out `http://bassistance.de/jquery-plugins/jquery-plugin-validation/` and consider making a donation to the project. It has made all of our lives better.

Now that we have properly integrated jQuery Validate into our multi-page form, we need to make our errors look like proper errors. We could go with something really simple, such as a red color on the text, but I much prefer keeping with the style of jQuery Mobile. Their default theme set has a `data-theme="e"` that is just begging to be used for error states. It might seem like a good idea to just add our error classes onto the very definitions of their `ui-bar-e`, but don't. jQuery Mobile was patched three times during the writing of this book and if we were to take that approach it would cause friction with every upgrade. Instead, let's just copy the definition of `ui-bar-e` right into our custom stylesheet, as shown in the following code:

```
label.error,input.error{
border:1px solid #f7c942;
background:#fadb4e;
color:#333;
text-shadow:0 1px 0 #fff;
background-image:-webkit-gradient(linear,lefttop,leftbottom,from(#fced
```

```
a7) ,to (#fbef7e) ) ;
background-image:-webkit-linear-gradient (#fceda7,#fbef7e) ;
background-image:-moz-linear-gradient (#fceda7,#fbef7e) ;
background-image:-ms-linear-gradient (#fceda7,#fbef7e) ;
background-image:-o-linear-gradient (#fceda7,#fbef7e) ;
background-image:linear-gradient (#fceda7,#fbef7e) }
```

We're almost ready to go with our fancy forms. Now we just need to be able to make it validated before moving from page to page. We don't have to worry about the submit link, as that will naturally trigger validation, but let's add a class to the continue link using the following code:

```
<a data-role="button" data-theme="b" href="#payment"
class="validateContinue">Continue</a>
```

Then, in our global scripts, let's add this function to our `pageinit` handler using the following code:

```
$page.find(".validateContinue").click(function(){
  if($(this).closest("form").data("validator").form()){
    return true;
  }else{
    event.stopPropagation();
    event.preventDefault();
    return false;
  }
});
```

What happens if the user refreshes in the middle of this process? The fields will be empty but we'll already be on to the next page. One little script at the bottom of the page, as shown in the following code, should handle that:

```
//page refresh mitigation
$(document).on("pagebeforeshow", function(){
  if(document.location.hash != ""){
    var $firstRequiredInput =
$("input.pageRequired").first();
    if($firstRequiredInput.val() == ""){
      var redirectPage =
$firstRequiredInput.closest("[data-role='page']");
      $.mobile.changePage(redirectPage);
    }
  }
});
```

Now that we have the basic concepts and have overcome a few minor pitfalls, let's see the finished code of the `ordercheckout.php` file:

```
<!DOCTYPE html>
<html>
<?php
  $documentTitle = "Check Out | Nicky's Pizza";

  $headerLeftHref = "";
  $headerLeftLinkText = "Back";
  $headerLeftIcon = "";

  $headerRightHref = "tel:8165077438";
  $headerRightLinkText = "Call";
  $headerRightIcon = "grid";

  $fullSiteLinkHref = "/";

?>
<head>
  <?php include("includes/meta.php"); ?>
  <style type="text/css">
    #ordernameContainer{display:none;}
  </style>
</head>

<body>
  <form action="thankyou.php" method="post" class="validateMe">
```

Here is the first page of our multi-page form. Remember that these pages will all be submitted at once. We'll be validating each page using the following code before the user can move to the next:

```
div data-role="page" id="delivery">
  <?php $headerTitle = "Deliver To"; ?>
  <?php include("includes/header.php"); ?>
  <div data-role="content">
    <h2>Where will we be delivering?</h2>

    <p>
      <label for="streetAddress">Street Address</label>
      <input type="text" name="streetAddress" id="streetAddress"
class="pageRequired" />
    </p>

    <p>
```

```
        <label for="streetAddress2">Address Line 2 | Apt#</label>
        <input type="text" name="streetAddress2" id="streetAddress2" />
      </p>

      <p>
        <label for="zip">Zip Code</label>
        <input type="number" name="zip" id="zip" maxlength="5"
  class="pageRequired zip" />
      </p>

      <p>
        <label for="phone">Phone Number</label>
        <input type="tel" name="phone" id="phone" maxlength="10"
  class="number pageRequired" />
      </p>

      <p>
        <div class="ui-grid-a">
          <div class="ui-block-a"><a data-role="button"
  data-icon="delete" data-iconpos="left" data-theme="d"
  href="javascript://">Cancel</a></div>
          <div class="ui-block-b"><a data-role="button" data-
  icon="arrow-r" data-iconpos="right" data-theme="b" href="#payment" cla
  ss="validateContinue">Continue</a></div>
        </div>
      </p>

    </div>
    <?php include("includes/footer.php"); ?>
  </div>
```

This is the second page of the form for collecting payment information. Note the validation of the credit card. All we have to do is add the class "creditcard" to make the framework check if the card number validates with the Luhn algorithm (http://en.wikipedia.org/wiki/Luhn_algorithm).

```
  <div data-role="page" id="payment">
    <?php $headerTitle = "Payment"; ?>
    <?php include("includes/header.php"); ?>
    <div data-role="content">
      <h2>Please enter payment information</h2>

      <p>
        <label for="nameOnCard">Name on card</label>
        <input type="text" name="nameOnCard" id="nameOnCard"
  class="pageRequired" />
      </p>
```

```
    <p>
      <label for="cardNumber">Card Number</label>
      <input type="tel" name="cardNumber" id="cardNumber"
  class="pageRequired creditcard" />
    </p>


    <p>
      <label for="expiration">Expiration</label>
      <input class="pageRequired number" type="tel" name="expiration"
id="expiration" maxlength="4" size="4" placeholder="MMYY" />
    </p>


    <p>
      <label for="cvv">CVV2 (on the back of your card)</label>
      <input class="pageRequired number" type="number" name="cvv"
id="cvv" minlength="3" maxlength="4" />
    </p>


    <p>
      <input type="checkbox" value="true" name="savePayment"
id="savePayment" /><label for="savePayment">Save payment info for
easier ordering?</label>
      <input type="checkbox" value="true" name="saveOrder"
id="saveOrder" onchange="showHideOrderNameContainer()" /><label
for="saveOrder">Save this order to your favorites?</label>
    </p>


    <p id="ordernameContainer">
      <label for="ordername">Give your order a name</label>
      <input type="text" name="ordername" id="ordername"
placeholder="example: the usual" />
    </p>


    <p>
      <div class="ui-grid-a">
        <div class="ui-block-a"><a data-role="button"
data-icon="delete" data-iconpos="left" data-theme="d"
href="javascript://">Cancel</a></div>
        <div class="ui-block-b"><input type="submit" data-
icon="arrow-r" data-iconpos="right" data-theme="b" value="Submit" /></
div>
      </div>
    </p>

  </div>
  <?php include("includes/footer.php"); ?>
</div>


</form>
```

These are the scripts we had mentioned earlier in the chapter:

```
<script type="text/javascript">
 function showHideOrderNameContainer(){
  if($("#saveOrder").attr("checked")){
   $("#ordernameContainer").show();
  }else{
   $("#ordernameContainer").hide();
  }
 }

 //page refresh mitigation
 $("[data-role='page']").live("pagebeforeshow", function(){
  if(document.location.hash != ""){
   var $firstRequiredInput = $("input.pageRequired").first();
   if($firstRequiredInput.val() == ""){
    var redirectPage = $firstRequiredInput.closest("[data-
role='page']");
    $.mobile.changePage(redirectPage);
   }
  }

 });
 </script>
</body>
</html>
```

Here is the `meta.php` file since integrating jQuery Validate:

```
<meta charset="utf-8">
<meta name="viewport" content="width=device-width, initial-scale=1,
maximum-scale=1.0, user-scalable=no">
<link href='http://fonts.googleapis.com/css?family=Marvel'
rel='stylesheet' type='text/css'>
<linkrel="stylesheet" href=
"http://code.jquery.com/mobile/1.2.0/jquery.mobile-1.2.0.min.css"
/>
<link rel="stylesheet" href="css/custom.css" />
<script src="http://code.jquery.com/jquery-1.8.2.min.js"></script>
<script src="js/jquery.cookie.js"></script>
<script src="js/jquery.validate.min.js"></script>
<script src="js/global.js"></script>
<script src="http://code.jquery.com/mobile/1.2.0/jquery.mobile-
1.2.0.min.js"></script>
<title><?=$documentTitle?></title>
```

After three chapters, here is what could conceivably be called the master JavaScript file (global.js). It is essentially the one I use in every project with only minor variations:

```
var _gaq = _gaq || [];
var GAID = 'UA-XXXXXXXX-X';



/*******************************************************/
/* Load Google Analytics only once the page is fully loaded.
/*******************************************************/
$(document).ready(function(e) {
(function() {
var ga = document.createElement('script');
ga.type = 'text/javascript';
ga.async = true;
ga.src = ('https:' == document.location.protocol ?
'https://ssl' : 'http://www')
  +'.google-analytics.com/ga.js';
var s = document.getElementsByTagName('script')[0];
s.parentNode.insertBefore(ga, s);
})();
});



/*******************************************************/
/* Upon jQM page initialization, place hooks on links with
/* data-pageview attributes to track more with GA.
/* Also, hook onto the full-site links to make them cookie
/* the user upon click.
/*******************************************************/
$(document).on('pageinit', function (event, ui) {
$page = $(event.target);

$page.find("[data-pageview]").click(function(){
var $eventTarget = $(this);
if($eventTarget.attr("data-pageview") == "href"){
_gaq.push(['_trackPageview',
$eventTarget.attr("href")]);
}else{
_gaq.push(['_trackPageview',
$eventTarget.attr("data-pageview")]);
}
});
```

```
$page.find("a.fullSiteLink").click(function(){
$.cookie("fullSiteClicked","true", {
path: "/",
expires:3600
});
});


/*****************************************************/
/* Find any form with the class of validateMe and hook in
/* jQuery Validate.  Also, override the error placement.
/*****************************************************/
//Any form that might need validation
$("form.validateMe").each(function(index, element) {
var $form = $(this);
var v = $form.validate({
errorPlacement: function(error, element) {
var dataErrorAt = element.attr("data-error-at"); if (dataErrorAt)
$(dataErrorAt).html(error);
else
error.insertBefore(element);
        }
});
});


/*****************************************************/
/* Hook in the validateContinue buttons.
/*****************************************************/
$page.find(".validateContinue").click(function(){
if($(this).closest("form").data("validator").form()){ return true;
}else{
event.stopPropagation();
event.preventDefault();
return false;
}
});
});


/*****************************************************/
/* Every time a page shows, register it in GA.
/*****************************************************/
```

```
$(document).on('pageshow', function (event, ui) {
try {
_gaq.push(['_setAccount', GAID]);
if ($.mobile.activePage.attr("data-url")) {
_gaq.push(['_trackPageview',
$.mobile.activePage.attr("data-url")]);
} else {
_gaq.push(['_trackPageview']);
    }
} catch(err) {}
});


/*********************************************************/
/*  Add the custom validator class to allow for validation
/*  on multi-page forms.
/*********************************************************/
$.validator.addMethod("pageRequired", function(value, element) {
var $element = $(element);
if( $element.closest("."+$.mobile.subPageUrlKey)
.hasClass($.mobile.activePageClass))
{
return !this.optional(element);
}
return "dependency-mismatch";
}, $.validator.messages.required);
```

E-commerce tracking with Google Analytics

So far, all we have tracked is page views. Very useful to be sure, but most managers and owners love their reports. On the Thank You page, we should include some simple e-commerce tracking. Again, because of jQuery Mobile's Ajax-based navigation system, we'll need to tweak the default examples just a hair to make it work perfectly with jQM.

Here is the full code for the Thank You page (thankyou.php) with e-commerce tracking set to only run once the page is shown:

```
<!DOCTYPE html>
<html>
<?php
  $documentTitle = "Menu | Nicky's Pizza";
```

```php
  $headerLeftHref = "index.php";
  $headerLeftLinkText = "Home";
  $headerLeftIcon = "home";

  $headerRightHref = "tel:8165077438";
  $headerRightLinkText = "Call";
  $headerRightIcon = "grid";

  $fullSiteLinkHref = "/index.php";
?>
<head>
  <?php include("includes/meta.php"); ?>
</head>

<body>
<div data-role="page" id="orderthankyou">
  <?php
    $headerTitle = "Thank you";
    include("includes/header.php");
  ?>
  <div data-role="content" >
    <h2>Thank you for your order. </h2>
    <p>In a few minutes, you should receive an email confirming your
order with an estimated delivery time.</p>

    <script type="text/javascript">
      $("#orderthankyou").live('pageshow', function(){
        _gaq.push(['_addTrans',
          '1234',                     // order ID - required
          'Mobile Checkout',   // affiliation or store name
          '21.99',                    // total - required
          '1.29',                     // tax
          ' ',                        // shipping
          'Kansas City',        // city
          'MO',                 // state or province
          'USA'                 // country
          ]);
        _gaq.push(['_trackTrans']); //submits transaction to the
 Analytics servers
      });
    </script>
  </div>
  <?php include("includes/footer.php"); ?>
</div>

</body>
</html>
```

Summary

Forms are nothing new. We've had them since the dawn of the Internet. They are not glamorous, but they can be elegant, effective, and responsive. jQuery Mobile takes you a long way toward effective forms in touch-based interfaces. Now you can take it farther with multi-page forms and client-side validation. Do not underestimate the power of these two techniques when paired together. When the client is able to do virtually everything they need, without having to go back to the server, the experience is automatically improved. Mixing in the ability to watch how users are surfing your site, their favorite content, and their fallout points will help you make an even more compelling experience. Just remember, when you're thinking about analytics, it is not the absolute numbers that are important. It's all about the trends; with these basics done, let's get to some more interesting tech. In the next chapter, we'll start looking at geolocation and more.

4

QR Codes, Geolocation, Google Maps API, and HTML5 Video

We have discussed many of the core concerns of small and big business. Let's turn our eyes now to other concepts that would concern media companies. In this chapter, we'll look at a movie theater chain, but really, these concepts could be applied to any business that has multiple physical locations.

In this chapter, we'll cover:

- QR Codes
- Basic geolocation
- Integrating Google Maps API
- Linking and embedding video

QR codes

We love our smartphones. We love showing off what our smartphones can do. So, when those cryptic squares, as shown in the following figure, started showing up all over the place and befuddling the masses, smartphone users quickly stepped up and started showing people what it's all about in the same overly-enthusiastic manner that we whip them out to answer even the most trivial question heard in passing. And, since it looks like NFC isn't taking off anytime soon, we'd better be familiar with QR codes and how to leverage them.

The data shows that knowledge and usage of QR codes is very high according to surveys:(`http://researchaccess.com/2012/01/new-data-on-qr-code-adoption/`)

- More than two-thirds of smartphone users have scanned a code
- More than 70 percent of the users say they'd do it again (especially for a discount)

Wait, what does this have to do with jQuery Mobile? Traffic. Big-time successful traffic. A banner ad is considered successful if only two percent of people click through (`http://en.wikipedia.org/wiki/Clickthrough_rate`). QR codes get more than 66 percent! I'd say it's a pretty good way to get people to our creations and, thus, should be of concern. But QR codes are for more than just URLs. Here we have a URL, a block of text, a phone number, and an SMS in the following QR codes:

There are many ways to generate QR codes (`http://www.the-qrcode-generator.com/`, `http://www.qrstuff.com/`). Really, just search for `QR Code Generator` on Google and you'll have numerous options.

Let us consider a local movie theater chain. Dickinson Theatres (`dtmovies.com`) has been around since the 1920s and is considering throwing its hat into the mobile ring. Perhaps they will invest in a mobile website, and go all-out in placing posters and ads in bus stops and other outdoor locations. Naturally, people are going to start scanning, and this is valuable to us because they're going to tell us exactly which locations are paying off. This is really a first in the advertising industry. We have a medium that seems to spur people to interact on devices that will tell us exactly where they were when they scanned it. Geolocation matters and this can help us find the right locations.

Geolocation

When GPS first came out on phones, it was pretty useless for anything other than police tracking in case of emergencies. Today, it is making the devices that we hold in our hands even more personal than our personal computers. For now, we can get a latitude, longitude, and timestamp very dependably. The geolocation API specification from the W3C can be found at `http://dev.w3.org/geo/api/spec-source.html`. For now, we'll pretend that we have a poster prompting the user to scan a QR code to find the nearest theater and show the timings. It would bring the user to a page like this:

Since there's no better first date than dinner and a movie, the movie going crowd tends to skew a bit to the younger side. Unfortunately, that group does not tend to have a lot of money. They may have more feature phones than smartphones. Some might only have very basic browsers. Maybe they have JavaScript, but we can't count on it. If they do, they might have geolocation. Regardless, given the audience, progressive enhancement is going to be the key.

The first thing we'll do is create a base level page with a simple form that will submit a zip code to a server. Since we're using our template from before, we'll add validation to the form for anyone who has JavaScript using the `validateMe` class. If they have JavaScript and geolocation, we'll replace the form with a message saying that we're trying to find their location. For now, don't worry about creating this file. The source code is incomplete at this stage. This page will evolve and the final version will be in the source package for the chapter in the file called `qrresponse.php` as shown in the following code:

```php
<?php
  $documentTitle = "Dickinson Theatres";
  $headerLeftHref = "/";
  $headerLeftLinkText = "Home";
  $headerLeftIcon = "home";

  $headerTitle = "";
  $headerRightHref = "tel:8165555555";
  $headerRightLinkText = "Call";
  $headerRightIcon = "grid";

  $fullSiteLinkHref = "/";
?>
<!DOCTYPE html>
<html>
<head>
  <?php include("includes/meta.php"); ?>
</head>
<body>
<div id="qrfindclosest" data-role="page">
  <div class="logoContainer ui-shadow"></div>
  <div data-role="content">
    <div id="latLong>
      <form id="findTheaterForm" action="fullshowtimes.php"
method="get" class="validateMe">
        <p>
```

```
            <label for="zip">Enter Zip Code</label>
            <input type="tel" name="zip" id="zip"
class="required number"/>
        </p>
        <p><input type="submit" value="Go"></p>
      </form>
    </div>
    <p>
      <ul id="showing" data-role="listview" class="movieListings"
data-dividertheme="g">
      </ul>
    </p>
  </div>
  <?php include("includes/footer.php"); ?>
</div>
<script type="text/javascript">
  //We'll put our page specific code here soon
</script>
</body>
</html>
```

For anyone who does not have JavaScript, this is what they will see, nothing special. We could spruce it up with a little CSS but what would be the point? If they're on a browser that doesn't have JavaScript, there's pretty good chance their browser is also miserable at rendering CSS. That's fine really. After all, progressive enhancement doesn't necessarily mean making it wonderful for everyone, it just means being sure it works for everyone. Most will never see this but if they do, it will work just fine.

For everyone else, we'll need to start working with JavaScript to get our theater data in a format we can digest programmatically. JSON is perfectly suited for this task. If you are already familiar with the concept of JSON, skip to the next paragraph now. If you're not familiar with it, basically, it's another way of shipping data across the Interwebs. It's like XML but more useful. It's less verbose and can be directly interacted with and manipulated using JavaScript because it's actually written in JavaScript. JSON is an acronym for JavaScript Object Notation. A special thank you goes out to Douglas Crockford (the father of JSON). XML still has its place on the server. It has no business in the browser as a data format if you can get JSON. This is such a widespread view that at the last developer conference I went to, one of the speakers chuckled as he asked, "Is anyone still actually using XML?"

The example code for this chapter has the full list of theaters, but this should be enough to get us started. For this example, we'll store the JSON data in /js/theaters.js.

```
{
    "theaters":[
        {
            "id":161,
            "name":"Chenal 9 IMAX Theatre",
            "address":"17825 Chenal Parkway",
            "city":"Little Rock",
            "state":"AR",
            "zip":"72223",
            "distance":9999,
            "geo":{"lat":34.7684775,"long":-92.4599322},
            "phone":"501-821-2616"
        },
        {
            "id":158,
            "name":"Gateway 12 IMAX Theatre",
            "address":"1935 S. Signal Butte",
            "city":"Mesa",
            "state":"AZ",
            "zip":"85209",
            "distance":9999,
            "geo":{"lat":33.3788674,"long":-111.6016081},
            "phone":"480-354-8030"
        },
        {
            "id":135,
            "name":"Northglen 14 Theatre",
            "address":"4900 N.E. 80th Street",
```

```
        "city":"Kansas City",
        "state":"MO",
        "zip":"64119",
        "distance":9999,
        "geo":{"lat":39.240027,"long":-94.5226432},
        "phone":"816-468-1100"
      }
  ]
}
```

Now that we have data to work with, we can prepare the on-page scripts. Let's put the following chunks of JavaScript in a script tag at the bottom of the HTML where we had the comment: We'll put our page specific code here soon.

```
//declare our global variables
var theaterData = null;
var timestamp = null;
var latitude = null;
var longitude = null;
var closestTheater = null;

//Once the page is initialized, hide the manual zip code form
//and place a message saying that we're attempting to find
//their location.
$(document).on("pageinit", "#qrfindclosest", function(){
  if(navigator.geolocation){
    $("#findTheaterForm").hide();
    $("#latLong").append("<p id='finding'>Finding your location...</p>");
  }
});

//Once the page is showing, go grab the theater data and find out
which one is closest.
$(document).on("pageshow", "#qrfindclosest", function(){
  theaterData = $.getJSON("js/theaters.js",
    function(data){
      theaterData = data;
      selectClosestTheater();
    });
});

function selectClosestTheater(){
  navigator.geolocation.getCurrentPosition(
  function(position) { //success
```

```
    latitude = position.coords.latitude;
    longitude = position.coords.longitude;
    timestamp = position.timestamp;
    for(var x = 0; x < theaterData.theaters.length; x++)
  {   var theater = theaterData.theaters[x];
       var distance = getDistance(latitude, longitude,
  theater.geo.lat, theater.geo.long);
       theaterData.theaters[x].distance = distance;
    }}
    theaterData.theaters.sort(compareDistances);
    closestTheater = theaterData.theaters[0];
      _gaq.push(['_trackEvent', "qr", "ad_scan",
  (""+latitude+","+longitude) ]);
   var dt = new Date();
   dt.setTime(timestamp);
   $("#latLong").html("<div class='theaterName'>"
     +closestTheater.name+"</div><strong>"
     +closestTheater.distance.toFixed(2)
     +"miles</strong><br/>"
     +closestTheater.address+"<br/>"
     +closestTheater.city+", "+closestTheater.state+" "
     +closestTheater.zip+"<br/><a href='tel:"
     +closestTheater.phone+"'>"
     +closestTheater.phone+"</a>");
   $("#showing").load("showtimes.php", function(){
     $("#showing").listview('refresh');
   });
 },
 function(error){ //error
   switch(error.code)
   {
     case error.TIMEOUT:
       $("#latLong").prepend("<div class='ui-bar-e'>
 Unable to get your position: Timeout</div>");
       break;
     case error.POSITION_UNAVAILABLE:
       $("#latLong").prepend("<div class='ui-bar-e'>
 Unable to get your position: Position unavailable</div>");
       break;
     case error.PERMISSION_DENIED:
       $("#latLong").prepend("<div class='ui-bar-e'>
 Unable to get your position: Permission denied.
 You may want to check your settings.</div>");
       break;
     case error.UNKNOWN_ERROR:
```

```
    $("#latLong").prepend("<div class='ui-bar-e'>
Unknown error while trying to access your position.</div>");
        break;
    }
    $("#finding").hide();
    $("#findTheaterForm").show();
},
{maximumAge:600000}); //nothing too stale
}
```

The key here is the function `geolocation.getCurrentPosition`, which will prompt the user to allow us access to their location data, as shown here on iPhone.

If somebody is ~~really paranoid~~ a privacy advocate, they may ~~be wearing a tin-foil hat~~ have turned off all location services. In this case, ~~they should probably not be using a cell phone~~ we'll need to inform the user that their choice has impacted our ability to help them. That's what the error function is all about. In such a case, we'll display an error message and show the standard form again.

Once we have our user's position and the list of theaters, it's time to sort the theaters by distance and show the closest one. The following is a pretty generic code that we may want to use on more than one page. So we'll put this into our `global.js` file:

```
function getDistance(lat1, lon1, lat2, lon2){
    //great-circle distances between the two points
    //because the earth isn't flat
    var R = 6371; // km
    var dLat = (lat2-lat1).toRad();
    var dLon = (lon2-lon1).toRad();
    var lat1 = lat1.toRad();
    var lat2 = lat2.toRad();
    var a = Math.sin(dLat/2) * Math.sin(dLat/2) +
```

```
      Math.sin(dLon/2) * Math.cos(lat1) *
      Math.cos(lat2);
    var c = 2 * Math.atan2(Math.sqrt(a), Math.sqrt(1-a));
    var d = R * c; //distance in km
    var m = d * 0.621371;  //distance in miles
    return m;
  }
  if (typeof(Number.prototype.toRad) === "undefined") {
    Number.prototype.toRad = function() {
      return this * Math.PI / 180;
    }
  }
}

function compareDistances(a,b) {
  if (a.distance<b.distance) return -1;
  if (a.distance>b.distance) return 1;
  return 0;
}
```

With all of these pieces in place, it is now simple enough to get the user's position and find the closest theater. It will be the first in the array, as well as stored directly in the global variable, `closestTheater`. If they have JavaScript turned off, we'll have to use some server-side algorithms or APIs to figure out which is closest (which is beyond the scope of this book). Regardless, we are keeping every theater's show times as a set of list items in a flat file (`showtimes.php`). In a real world situation, this would be database driven and we would call the page with a URL that has the ID of the correct theater. For now, the following code is all we need:

```
<li data-role="list-divider">Opening This Week</li>
<li>
  <a href="movie.php?id=193818">
    <img src="images/darkknightrises.jpeg">
    <h3>Dark Knight Rises</h3>
    <p>PG-13 - 2h 20m<br/>
      <strong>Showtimes:</strong>
      12:00 - 12:30 - 1:00 - 1:30 - 3:30 - 4:00 - 4:30 -
      7:00 - 7:15 - 7:30 - 7:45 - 8:00 - 10:30 - 10:45
    </p>
  </a>
</li>
<li>
  <a href="moviedetails.php?id=193812">
    <img src="images/iceagecontinentaldrift.jpeg">
    <h3>Ice Age 4: Continental Drift</h3>
    <p>PG - 1h 56m<br/>
```

```
        <strong>Showtimes:</strong> 10:20 AM - 10:50 AM -
        12:40 - 1:15 - 3:00 - 7:00 - 7:30 - 9:30
      </p>
    </a>
  </li>
  <li data-role="list-divider">Also in Theaters</li>
  <li>
    <a href="moviedetails.php?id=194103">
      <img src="images/savages.jpeg">
      <h3>Savages</h3>
      <p>R - 7/6/2012<br/><strong>Showtimes:</strong>
        10:05 AM - 1:05 - 4:05 - 7:05 - 10:15
      </p>
    </a>
  </li>
  <li>
    <a href="moviedetails.php?id=194226">
      <img src="images/katyperrypartofme.jpeg">
      <h3>Katy Perry: Part of Me</h3>
      <p>PG - 7/5/2012<br/>
        <strong>Showtimes:</strong> 10:05 AM - 1:05 -
        4:05 - 7:05 - 10:15
      </p>
    </a>
  </li>
  <li>
    <a href="moviedetails.php?id=193807">
      <img src="images/amazingspiderman.jpeg">
      <h3>Amazing Spider-Man</h3>
      <p>PG-13 - 7/5/2012<br/>
        <strong>Showtimes:</strong> 10:00 AM - 1:00 -
        4:00 - 7:00 - 10:00
      </p>
    </a>
  </li>
```

We pull in this page fragment using the following on-page scripts:

```
$("#showing").load("showtimes.php", function(){
    $("#showing").listview('refresh');
});
```

In this case we have the `showtimes.php` file containing only the listview items, and we are injecting them directly into the listview before refreshing. Another way to accomplish the same thing would be to have another file, like `fullshowtimes.php`, be a fully rendered page with headers, footers, and everything. This would be perfect for the situations where JavaScript or geolocation is not available and we have to revert back to standard page submissions.

```php
<?php
  $documentTitle = "Showtimes | Northglen 16 Theatre";
  $headerLeftHref = "/";
  $headerLeftLinkText = "Home";
  $headerLeftIcon = "home";
  $headerTitle = "";
  $headerRightHref = "tel:8165555555";
  $headerRightLinkText = "Call";
  $headerRightIcon = "grid";
  $fullSiteLinkHref = "/";
?>
<!DOCTYPE html>
<html>
<head>
  <?php include("includes/meta.php"); ?>
</head>
<body>
  <div id="qrfindclosest" data-role="page">
    <div class="logoContainer ui-shadow"></div>
    <div data-role="content">
      <h3>Northglen 14 Theatre</h3>

      <p><a href="https://maps.google.com/maps?q=Northglen+14+Theatre,
+Northeast+80th+Street,,+Kansas+City,+MO&hl=en&sll=38.304661,
-92.437099&sspn=7.971484,8.470459&oq=northglen+&t=h&hq=Northglen+
14+Theatre,&hnear=NE+80th+St,+Kansas+City,+Clay,
+Missouri&z=15">4900 N.E. 80th Street<br>
```

```
            Kansas City, MO 64119</a>
        </p>

        <p><a href="tel:8164681100">816-468-1100</a></p>
        <p>
          <ul id="showing" data-role="listview"
   class="movieListings" data-dividertheme="g">
              <?php include("includes/showtimes.php"); ?>
          </ul>
        </p>
      </div>
      <?php include("includes/footer.php");?>
    </div>
  </body>
</html>
```

Then, instead of calling the load function with simply a page, we could load the entire page and then select the elements in the page we want to inject by using the following code:

```
$("#showing").load("fullshowtimes.php #showing li", function(){
  $("#showing").listview('refresh');
});
```

Certainly, this would be a less efficient way of doing things, but it's worth noting that such a thing can be done. It almost certainly will come in handy in the future.

Integrating the Google Maps API

We've done well up to this point on our own. We can tell which theater is closest and how far it is as the crow flies. Sadly though, despite all it's promise, the 21st century has not led to us all having private jet packs. Therefore, it is probably best that we not display that distance. Most likely, they're going to drive, ride a bus, bike, or walk.

Let's leverage the Google Maps API (`https://developers.google.com/maps/documentation/javascript/`). If your site is going to have a lot of API hits, you might have to pay for the business pricing. For us, while we are in development, there's no need.

Here's a look at what we're about to build:

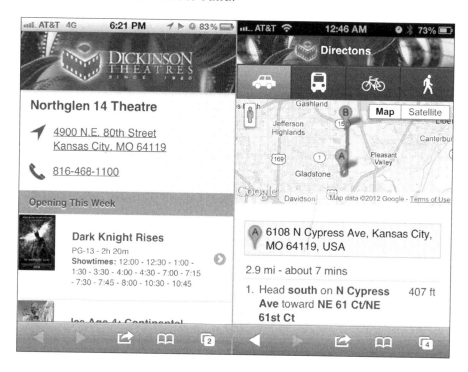

First, we'll need another page to show a map and directions, as well as the script that will actually load the maps from Google Maps API, using the following code:

```
<div id="directions" data-role="page">
  <div data-role="header">
    <h3>Directions</h3>
  </div>
  <div data-role="footer">
    <div data-role="navbar" class="directionsBar">
      <ul>
        <li>
          <a href="#" id="drivingButton"
onClick="showDirections('DRIVING')">
            <div class="icon driving"></div>
          </a>
        </li>
        <li>
          <a href="#" id="transitButton"
onClick="showDirections('TRANSIT')">
            <div class="icon transit"></div>
          </a>
```

```
            </li>
            <li>
              <a href="#" id="bicycleButton"
 onClick="showDirections('BICYCLING')">
                  <div class="icon bicycle"></div>
              </a>
            </li>
            <li>
              <a href="#" id="walkingButton"
 onClick="showDirections('WALKING')">
                  <div class="icon walking"></div>
              </a>
            </li>
          </ul>
        </div>
      </div>
      <div id="map_canvas"></div>
      <div data-role="content" id="directions-panel">
      </div>
    </div>
    <script
 src="https://maps.googleapis.com/maps/api/js?sensor=true">
    </script>
```

We have several important parts of this page. The first is the `navbar` attribute within a `footer` attribute for directions to the theater. What you may not realize is that footers don't actually have to be at the bottom of the page. When you use a `navbar` attribute within a `footer` attribute, the link that you clicked on will retain its active state. Without the footer surrounding it, the link will only blink the active state once and then go back to normal. The `map_canvas` and `directions-panel` attributes will be filled in by the Google Maps API.

Now, we need to update the CSS code for the extra icons and map constraints. As before, we're keeping them in the location `/css/custom.css`.

```
.directionsBar .icon{
  height:28px;
  width:34px;
  margin:auto;
  background-repeat:no-repeat;
  background-position:center center;
}

.directionsBar .driving{
  background-image:url(../icons/xtras-white/16-car.png);
```

```css
    background-size:34px 19px;
  }
  .directionsBar .transit{
    background-image:url(../icons/xtras-white/15-bus.png);
    background-size:22px 28px;
  }
  .directionsBar .bicycle{
    background-image:url(../icons/xtras-white/13-bicycle.png);
    background-size:34px 21px;
  }
  .directionsBar .walking{
    background-image:url(../icons/icons-white/102-walk.png);
    background-size:14px 27px;
  }
  .theaterAddress{
    padding-left:35px;
    background-image:url(../icons/icons-gray/193-location-arrow.png);
    background-size:24px 24px;
    background-repeat:no-repeat;
  }
  .theaterPhone{
    padding-left:35px;
    background-image:url(../icons/icons-gray/75-phone.png);
    background-size:24px 24px;
    background-repeat:no-repeat;
    height: 24px;
  }

  #map_canvas { height: 150px; }

  @media only screen and (-webkit-min-device-pixel-ratio: 1.5),
    only screen and (min--moz-device-pixel-ratio: 1.5),
    only screen and (min-resolution: 240dpi) {
      .directionsBar .driving{
        background-image:url(../icons/xtras-white/16-car@2x.png);
      }
      .directionsBar .transit{
        background-image:url(../icons/xtras-white/15-bus@2x.png);
      }
      .directionsBar .bicycle{
        background-image:url(../icons/xtras-white/13
bicycle@2x.png);
      }
      .directionsBar .walking{
```

```
        background-image:url(../icons/icons-white/102-walk@2x.png);
    }
    .theaterAddress{
        background-image:url(../icons/icons-gray/
193-location-arrow@2x.png);
    }
    .theaterPhone{
        background-image:url(../icons/icons-gray/75-phone@2x.png);
    }
}
```

Next, we'll add a few more global variables and functions to our current on-page scripts.

```
var directionData = null;
var directionDisplay;
var directionsService = new google.maps.DirectionsService();
var map;

function showDirections(travelMode){
  var request = {
    origin:latitude+","+longitude,
    destination:closestTheater.geo.lat+","
       +closestTheater.geo.long,
    travelMode: travelMode
  };

  directionsService.route(request,
    function(response, status){
      if (status == google.maps.DirectionsStatus.OK){
        directionsDisplay.setDirections(response);
      }
    });

  $("#directions").live("pageshow",
    function(){
      directionsDisplay = new google.maps.DirectionsRenderer();
      var userLocation = new google.maps.LatLng(latitude, longitude);
      var mapOptions = {
        zoom:14,
        mapTypeId: google.maps.MapTypeId.ROADMAP,
        center: userLocation
      }
      map = new google.maps.Map(
        document.getElementById('map_canvas'), mapOptions);
```

```
                directionsDisplay.setMap(map);
                directionsDisplay.setPanel(
                document.getElementById('directions-panel')
            );
            showDirections(
            google.maps.DirectionsTravelMode.DRIVING
        );
        $("#drivingButton").click();
    });
```

Here, we see the global variables for holding the Google objects. The showDirections method is made to take a string representing one of four different travel modes: 'DRIVING', 'TRANSIT', 'BICYCLING', and 'WALKING'.

We could populate the map and directions at the same time we figure out which theater is closest. It would actually make for a great user experience. However, without analytics to show that the majority of people actually want directions, it makes no sense to incur the costs. Ultimately, that is a business decision, but a company with a customer base of any size could get hammered with API costs. For now, it seems best to trigger the loading of maps and directions when the users go to the directions page.

Geek-out moment—GPS monitoring

So, let's geek-out for a minute. What we've done is probably good enough for most circumstances. We show a map and turn-by-turn directions. Let's take it a step further. The geolocation API does more than just determine your current location. It includes a timestamp (no biggie) and can allow you to continuously monitor the user's position using the method navigator.geolocation.watchPosition (http://dev.w3.org/geo/api/spec-source.html#watch-position). This means that with only a little bit of effort, we can turn our previous direction page into a continuously-updating directions page. In the example code, this is all contained within the file qrresponse2.php.

Again, updating too often could get expensive. So we should really limit how often we redraw the map and directions. For each transportation mode, there is a difference in the amount of meaningful time needed between updates. While we're at it, let's re-do the buttons to contain these options. Here is the entire page's code:

```php
<?php
    $documentTitle = "Dickinson Theatres";

    $headerLeftHref = "/";
    $headerLeftLinkText = "Home";
```

```php
  $headerLeftIcon = "home";

  $headerTitle = "";

  $headerRightHref = "tel:8165555555";
  $headerRightLinkText = "Call";
  $headerRightIcon = "grid";

  $fullSiteLinkHref = "/";
?>
<!DOCTYPE html>
<html>
<head>
  <?php include("includes/meta.php"); ?>
  <style type="text/css">
    .logoContainer{
      display:block;
      height:84px;
      background-image:url(images/header.png);
      background-position:top center;
      background-size:885px 84px;
      background-repeat:no-repeat;
    }
  </style>
  <script type="text/javascript"
src="http://maps.googleapis.com/maps/api/js?
key=asdfafefaewfacaevaeaceebvaewaewbk&sensor=true"></script>
</head>
<body>
  <div id="qrfindclosest" data-role="page">
    <div class="logoContainer ui-shadow"></div>
    <div data-role="content">
      <div id="latLong">
        <form id="findTheaterForm" action="fullshowtimes.php"
method="get" class="validateMe">
          <p>
            <label for="zip">Enter Zip Code</label>
            <input type="tel" name="zip" id="zip"
class="required number"/>
          </p>
          <p><input type="submit" value="Go"></p>
        </form>
      </div>
      <p>
        <ul id="showing" data-role="listview"
```

```
  class="movieListings" data-dividertheme="g">
        </ul>
      </p>
    </div>
    <?php include("includes/footer.php"); ?>
  </div>


  <div id="directions" data-role="page">
    <div data-role="header">
      <h3>Directions</h3>
    </div>
    <div data-role="footer">
      <div data-role="navbar" class="directionsBar">
        <ul>
          <li>
            <a href="#" id="drivingButton"
 data-transMode="DRIVING" data-interval="10000">
              <div class="icon driving"></div>
            </a>
          </li>
          <li>
            <a href="#" id="transitButton"
 data-transMode="TRANSIT" data-interval="10000">
              <div class="icon transit"></div>
            </a>
          </li>
          <li>
            <a href="#" id="bicycleButton"
 data-transMode="BICYCLING" data-interval="30000">
              <div class="icon bicycle"></div>
            </a>
          </li>
          <li>
            <a href="#" id="walkingButton"
 data-transMode="WALKING" data-interval="60000">
              <div class="icon walking"></div>
            </a>
          </li>
        </ul>
      </div>
    </div>
    <div id="map_canvas"></div>
    <div data-role="content" id="directions-panel"></div>
  </div>
```

So, now let's look at the on-page scripts for this GPS monitoring edition:

```
<script type="text/javascript">
  //declare our global variables
  var theaterData = null;
  var timestamp = null;
  var latitude = null;
  var longitude = null;
  var closestTheater = null;
  var directionData = null;
  var directionDisplay;
  var directionsService = new
    google.maps.DirectionsService();
  var map;
  var positionUpdateInterval = null;
  var transporationMethod = null;

  //Once the page is initialized, hide the manual zip form
  //and place a message saying that we're attempting to find
their location.
  $(document).on("pageinit", "#qrfindclosest", function(){
    if(navigator.geolocation){
      $("#findTheaterForm").hide();
      $("#latLong").append("<p id='finding'>Finding your
        location...</p>");

    }
  });

  $(document).on("pageshow", "#qrfindclosest", function(){
    theaterData = $.getJSON("js/theaters.js",
      function(data){
        theaterData = data;
        selectClosestTheater();
  });

    $("div.directionsBar a").click(function(){
      if(positionUpdateInterval != null){
        clearInterval(positionUpdateInterval);
      }
      var $link = $(this);
      transporationMethod = $link.attr("data-transMode");
      showDirections();
      setInterval(function(){
```

```
            showDirections();
        },Number($link.attr("data-interval")));
});

function showDirections(){
  var request = {
    origin:latitude+","+longitude,
      destination:closestTheater.geo.lat+","
      +closestTheater.geo.long,
    travelMode: transportationMethod
  }

  directionsService.route(request,
    function(response, status) {
      if (status == google.maps.DirectionsStatus.OK)
{     directionsDisplay.setDirections(response);
      }
  });
}

$(document).on("pageshow", "#directions", function(){
  directionsDisplay = new google.maps.DirectionsRenderer();
  var userLocation = new google.maps.LatLng(latitude, longitude);
  var mapOptions = {
    zoom:14,
    mapTypeId: google.maps.MapTypeId.ROADMAP,
    center: userLocation
  }
  map = new google.maps.Map(document.getElementById('map_canvas'),
mapOptions);
  directionsDisplay.setMap(map);
  directionsDisplay.setPanel(
    document.getElementById('directions-panel'));
  if(positionUpdateInterval == null) {
    transportationMethod = "DRIVING";
    positionUpdateInterval = setInterval(function(){
      showDirections();
    },(10000));
  }
  $("#drivingButton").click();
});

function selectClosestTheater(){
  var watchId=navigator.geolocation.watchPosition(
```

```
function(position){ //success
latitude = position.coords.latitude;
longitude = position.coords.longitude;
timestamp = position.timestamp;
var dt = new Date();
dt.setTime(timestamp);

for(var x = 0; x < theaterData.theaters.length; x++){
  var theater = theaterData.theaters[x];
  var distance = getDistance(latitude, longitude,
    theater.geo.lat, theater.geo.long);
  theaterData.theaters[x].distance = distance;          }

theaterData.theaters.sort(compareDistances);
closestTheater = theaterData.theaters[0];

$("#latLong").html("<div class='theaterName'>"
  +closestTheater.name
  +"</div><p class='theaterAddress'>
<a href='#directions'>"
  +closestTheater.address+"<br/>"
  +closestTheater.city+", "
  +closestTheater.state
  +" "+closestTheater.zip
  +"</a></p><p class='theaterPhone'><a href='tel:"
  +closestTheater.phone+"'>"
  +closestTheater.phone+"</a></p>"
);

$("#showing").load("fullshowtimes.php #showing li",
  function(){
    $("#showing").listview('refresh');
  });
  }
},
function(error){ //error
  $("#findTheaterForm").show();
  $("#finding").hide();
  switch(error.code) {
    case error.TIMEOUT:
      $("#latLong").prepend("<div class='ui-bar-e'>
Unable to get your position: Timeout</div>");
      break;
    case error.POSITION_UNAVAILABLE:
```

```
        $("#latLong").prepend("<div class='ui-bar-e'>
Unable to get your position: Position unavailable</div>");
        break;
     case error.PERMISSION_DENIED:
        $("#latLong").prepend("<div class='ui-bar-e'>
Unable to get your position: Permission denied.
You may want to check your settings.</div>");
        break;
     case error.UNKNOWN_ERROR:
        $("#latLong").prepend("<div class='ui-bar-e'>
Unknown error while trying to access your position.</div>");
        break;
   }
 });
}
</script>
</body>
</html>
```

Linking and embedding video

Previews are a staple in the movie industry. We could simply link directly to the previews on YouTube as many do. Here's a simple way to do it:

```
<p><a data-role="button"
href="http://www.youtube.com/watch?v=J9DlV9qwtF0">
Watch Preview</a></p>
```

That will work but the problem is that it takes the user away from your site. While that may not be the end of the world from a user's perspective, it's a big e-commerce no-no.

So, in order to improve the experience and keep the user on our own site, let's directly embed the HTML5 video and use the universal image for movie previews as we have depicted here.

Despite the fact that it looks like this will play in a teeny-tiny segment of the page, on smartphones, the video will play in fullscreen landscape mode. The story is a little different on the iPad where it will play inline at the embedded side.

Ultimately, we'd like to push the right-sized video back to the user for their device using the following code. Smartphones without high-resolution displays aren't exactly going to benefit from a 720p video.

```
<video id="preview" width="100%" controls
poster="images/preview.gif">

  <source src="previews/batmanTrailer-2_720.mp4" type="video/mp4"
media="only screen and (-webkit-min-device-pixel-ratio: 1.5),
only screen and (min--moz-device-pixel-ratio: 1.5),
only screen and (min-resolution: 240dpi)"/>

  <source src="previews/batmanTrailer-1_480.mov"
type="video/mov" />

  <a data-role="button"
href="http://www.youtube.com/watch?v=J9DlV9qwtF0">
Watch Preview</a>

</video>
```

If the browser recognizes the HTML5 video tag, the player will start at the top and look through each source tag until it finds one that it knows how to play and matches the right media query (if media queries have been specified). If the browser does not support HTML5 video, it will not know what to do with the video and source tags, and simply consider them to be valid XML elements. They will be treated like extraneous div tags and the link button will be displayed.

As you can see, we've added media queries here to different sources. If it's a high-resolution screen, we'll load a prettier video. You could really geek out here by adding lots of different sources: a 480p video for the average smartphone, a 720p video for the iPhone and early iPads, and a 1080p video for the 3rd generation iPad. The only word of caution here is that even though the Apple Retina Display is capable of showing a much more beautiful video, it still has to come over the same pipes. Loading a smaller video might still be better because it will play sooner and cost the customer less bandwidth.

Let's add a little more CSS to this picture. We're leaving the width at 100 percent of whatever is containing it. On smartphones, the picture ratio will scale properly as the width increases. The iPad, not so much. So, let's detect its screen resolutions using media queries and give it an explicit height that will take better advantage of the real estate.

```
/* iPad ---------------*/ @media only screen and
(min-device-width: 768px) and (max-device-width: 1024px) {
  #preview{ height:380px;}
}
```

Summary

We've explored the boundaries of modern media on smartphones. You can now brainstorm on the uses and take advantage of QR codes, find out where the user is, monitor the user's position, get directions and maps from Google, and feed responsive videos to the user.

Think about all you have just learned. How hard would it be to create a socially connected website that would allow users to get maps to each other's positions that continue to update as they move closer or further apart. It could be valuable if packaged and marketed properly.

In the next chapter, we're going to leverage GPS to pull tweets within your geographic area. We'll also look at pulling feeds from several other sources such as reddit, RSS feeds, and likewise. It's going to be a lot of fun. It was one of my favorite chapters to write.

5
Client-side Templating, JSON APIs, and HTML5 Web Storage

We've come a long way already and we've got some pretty hefty default templates and boilerplates for business. In this chapter, we're going to simplify and focus on some other things. We are going to create an aggregating news site based off social media. Until now, we've paid close attention to progressive enhancement. For this chapter, we leave that behind. This will require JavaScript.

In this chapter you will learn the following:

- Client-side templating options
- JsRender
- Patching into JSON API (Twitter)
- Programmatically changing pages
- Generated pages and DOM weight management
- Leveraging RSS feeds (natively)
- HTML5 Web Storage
- Leveraging the Google Feeds API

Client-side templating

(In a grumpy old man's voice) Back in my day, we rendered all the pages on the server, and we liked it! LOL! Times are changing and we are seeing a massive ground swell in client-side templating frameworks. At their heart, they're pretty much all the same in that they take JSON data and apply an HTML-based template contained within a script tag.

If you know what **JSON** is, skip this paragraph. I spent a little time last chapter discussing this, but just in case you skipped ahead and don't know, JSON is JavaScript written in such a way that it can be used as a data exchange format. It's more efficient than XML and is instantly interpretable by the browser in an object-oriented fashion. JSON can request data even across domains using JSONP. For more on JSON, read `http://en.wikipedia.org/wiki/JSON`. For more on JSONP, read `http://en.wikipedia.org/wiki/JSONP`.

All these client-side libraries have some sort of notation in them to show where the data goes and gives ways to implement looping and conditionals. Some are "logic-less" and operate on the philosophy that there should be as little logic as possible. If you subscribe to this wonderfully academic approach, good for you.

Honestly, from a purely pragmatic perspective, I believe that the template is the perfect place for code. The more flexible, the better. JSON holds the data and the templates are used to transform it. To draw a parallel, XML is the data format and XSL templates are used to transform. Nobody whines about logic in XSL; so, I don't see why it should be a problem in JS templates. But, all of this discussion is purely academic. In the end, they'll pretty much all do what you're looking for. If you're more of a designer than a coder, you may want to look more at the logic-less templates.

Following is a fairly exhaustive list of client-side templating frameworks. I'll probably miss a few and there will inevitably be more by the time this book gets published, but it's a start.

- doT
- dust.js
- Eco
- EJS
- Google Closure Templates
- handlebars

- haml-js

- kite

- Jade

- jQote2

- jQuery templates (discontinued)

- jsRender / jsView

- Parrot

- node-asyncEJS

- Nun

- Mu

- mustache

- montage

- Stencil

- underscore.js

Now, call me a fanboy, but, if it's officially jQuery, I love it. So, the first thing I tried was **jQuery Templates**. Sadly, shortly after learning to love it, the jQuery team abandoned the project and pointed people to **JsRender** as the continuation of the project. Whether that will be the continued direction in the future is another question, but, in the mean time, the features and power of JsRender make it a compelling offering and the basis for template work for the rest of this chapter. Not to mention, it's only 14k minified and fast as lightning. You can download the latest edition from `https://github.com/BorisMoore/jsrender`.

If you're looking for help to make the decision on the right template framework for you, Andy Matthews was kind enough to offer the following link during the review process for this chapter: `http://garann.github.com/template-chooser/`. It discusses the merits of several frameworks to help you make an informed choice. Thanks, Andy!

Patching into JSON APIs (Twitter)

It's always fun to watch the trending topics on Twitter. It, like so many other popular online destinations, has a JSON API. Let's have some fun. Here's what we're going to build. You can see the listview on the left-side and the search view on the right-side.

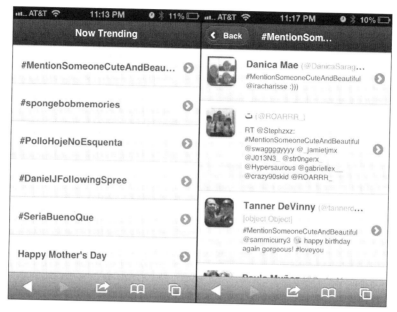

At this point, I'm going to dispense with the academically correct practice of separating the CSS and JS from the HTML. Aside from the libraries, all page-specific code (HTML, CSS, and JS) will be located within the single page. The following code is our starting base page. It is `twitter.html` in the code bundle for the chapter:

```
<!DOCTYPE html>
<html>
  <head>
    <meta charset="utf-8">
    <meta name="viewport" content="width=device-width, initial-
scale=1, maximum-scale=1.0, user-scalable=no">
    <title>Chapter 5 - News</title>
    <link rel="stylesheet" href="http://code.jquery.com/mobile/1.3.0/
jquery.mobile-1.3.0.min.css" />
    <script src="http://code.jquery.com/jquery-1.8.2.min.js"></script>
    <script src="js/jsrender.min.js" type="text/javascript"></script>
  <script src="http://code.jquery.com/mobile/1.3.0/jquery.mobile-
1.3.0.min.js"></script>
```

This next bit of styling will help our Twitter results look more Twitter-ish:

```css
<style type="text/css">
    .twitterItem .ui-li-has-thumb .ui-btn-inner a.ui-link-inherit,
#results .ui-li-static.ui-li-has-thumb{
        min-height: 50px;
        padding-left: 70px;
    }
    .twitterItem .ui-li-thumb, #results .ui-listview .ui-li-icon,
#results .ui-li-content{
        margin-top: 10px;
        margin-left: 10px;
    }
    .twitterItem .ui-li-desc{
        white-space:normal;
        margin-left:-25px;
    }
    .twitterItem .handle{
        font-size:80%;
        font-weight:normal;
        color:#aaa;
    }
    .twitterItem .ui-li-heading{
        margin: 0 0 .6em -25px;
    }
</style>
</head>
<body>
```

This page is pretty much just a placeholder that will be filled in once we get back results from hitting the Twitter API:

```html
<div id="home_page" data-role="page">
  <div data-role="header"><h1>Now Trending</h1></div>
  <div data-role="content">
    <ul id="results" data-role="listview" data-dividertheme="b">
    </ul>
  </div>
</div>
```

The following script is the processing core of the page.

```javascript
<script type="text/javascript">
    $(document).on("pagebeforeshow", "#home_page", function(){

        //before we show the page, go get the trending topics
```

```
      //from twitter
    $.ajax({
      url:"https://api.twitter.com/1/trends/daily.json",
        dataType:"jsonp",
        success: function(data) {
          var keys = Object.keys(data.trends);

          //Invoke jsRender on the template and pass in
          //the data to be used in the rendering.
          var content = $("#twitterTendingTemplate")
            .render(data.trends[keys[0]]);

          //Inject the rendered content into the results area
          //and refresh the listview
          $("#results").html( content ).listview("refresh");
        }
      })
      .error(function(jqXHR, textStatus, errorThrown){
        alert(textStatus+" - "+errorThrown);
      });
    });


  $(document).on('click', 'a.twitterSearch', function(){
    var searchTerm = $(this).attr("data-search");

    //take the search term from the clicked element and
    //do a search with the Twitter API
    $.ajax({
      url:"http://search.twitter.com/search.json?q="+escape
(searchTerm),
        dataType:"jsonp",
        success: function(data){

          //create a unique page ID based on the search term
          data.pageId = searchTerm.replace(/[# ]*/g,"");
          //add the search term to the data object
          data.searchTerm = searchTerm;

          //render the template with JsRender and the data
          var content = $("#twitterSearchPageTemplate").render(data);

          //The rendered content is a full jQuery Mobile
          //page with a unique ID.  Append it directly to the
          //body element
```

```
         $(document.body).append(content);

         //switch to the newly injected page
         $.mobile.changePage("#"+data.pageId);
      }
    })
    .error(function(jqXHR, textStatus, errorThrown){
      alert(textStatus+" - "+errorThrown);
    });
  });
</script>
```

Following are the two JsRender templates:

```
<script id="twitterTendingTemplate" type="text/x-jsrender">
  <li class="trendingItem">
    <a href="javascript://" class="twitterSearch" data-
search="{{>name}}">
      <h3>{{>name}}</h3>
    </a>
  </li>
</script>
```

```
<script id="twitterSearchPageTemplate" type="text/x-jsrender">
  <div id="{{>pageId}}" data-role="page" data-add-back-btn="true">
    <div data-role="header">
      <h1>{{>searchTerm}}</h1>
    </div>
    <div data-role="content">
      <ul id="results" data-role="listview" data-dividertheme="b">
        {{for results}}
          <li class="twitterItem">
            <a href="http://twitter.com/{{>from_user}}">
              <img src="{{>profile_image_url}}" alt="{{>from_user_
name}}" class="ui-shadow ui-corner-all" />
              <h3>{{>from_user_name}}
                <span class="handle">
                  (@{{>from_user}})<br/>
                  {{>location}}
                  {{if geo}}
                    {{>geo}}
                  {{/if}}
                </span>
              </h3>
              <p>{{>text}}</p>
```

```
          </a>
        </li>
      {{/for}}
    </ul>
  </div>
 </div>
</script>
</body>
</html>
```

OK, that was a lot of code to throw at you all at once, but most of it should look pretty familiar at this point. Let's start with explaining some of the newest stuff.

Normally, to pull data into a web page, you are subject to the same-domain policy even when you're pulling JSON. However, if it's coming from another domain, you'll need to bypass the same-domain policy. To bypass the some-domain policy, you could use some sort of server-side proxy such as PHP's **cURL** (http://php.net/manual/en/book.curl.php) or the Apache **HTTP Core Components** (http://hc.apache.org/) in the Java world.

Let's just keep things simple and use **JSONP** (also known as **JSON with Padding**). JSONP does not use a normal Ajax request to pull information. Despite the fact that the configuration options are for the $.ajax command, behind the scenes, it will execute the call for the data as a standalone script tag as follows:

```
<script type="text/javascript" src=" https://
api.twitter.com/1/trends/daily.json?callback=jQue
ry17200315623809584851_1345608708562&_=1345608708657"></script>
```

It is worth noting that JSONP is called using a GET request. That means that you can't use it to pass sensitive data, because it would be instantly viewable through network traffic scanning or simply looking at a browser's request history. So, no logging in over JSONP or passing anything sensitive. Got it?!

Before the actual request is made, jQuery will create a semi-random function name that will be executed once the response is received from the server. By appending that function name as the callback within the URL, we are telling Twitter to wrap their response to us with this function call. So, instead of receiving JSON script like {"trends": …}, we have a script written to our page that starts as follows:

```
jQuery17200315623809584851_1345608708562({"trends": …}).
```

The reason this works is because the same-domain policy does not exist for scripts. Handy, yes? After the script is loaded and the callback has processed, we will have the data in JSON format. In the end, the execution under the sheets is vastly different, but the results are the same as you would get with regular getJSON requests from your own domain.

Here is a slice of the response back from Twitter:

```
jQuery1720026425381423905492_1345774796764({
  "as_of": 1345774741,
  "trends": {
    "2012-08-23 05:20": [
      {
        "events": null,
        "name": "#ThingsISayTooMuch",
        "query": "#ThingsISayTooMuch",
        "promoted_content": null
      },
      {
        "events": null,
        "name": "#QuieroUnBesoDe",
        "query": "#QuieroUnBesoDe",
        "promoted_content": null
      },
      {
        "events": null,
        "name": "#ASongIKnowAllTheLyricsTo",
        "query": "#ASongIKnowAllTheLyricsTo",
        "promoted_content": null
      },
```

Next, we whittle down the response to only the part we want (the very latest set of trending topics) and pass that array into JsRender for ... well... rendering. It may seem more simple to just loop through the JSON and use string concatenation to build your output but take a look at the following template and tell me that's not going to be a lot cleaner to read and maintain:

```
<script id="twitterTendingTemplate" type="text/x-jsrender">
  <li class="trendingItem">
    <a href="javascript://" class="twitterSearch" data-
search="{{>name}}">
      <h3>{{>name}}</h3>
    </a>
  </li>
</script>
```

The `text/x-jsrender` type on the script will ensure that the page does not try to parse the inner contents as JavaScript. Since we passed in an array to JsRender, the template will be written for every object in the array. Now that is simple! Granted, we're only pulling the name out of the data object, but you get the idea of how this works.

Let's look at the next significant block of JavaScript:

```
$(document).on('click', "a.twitterSearch", function(){
  //grab the search term off the link
  var searchTerm = $(this).attr("data-search");

  //do a Twitter search based on that term
  $.ajax({        url:"http://search.twitter.com/search.json?q=
"+escape(searchTerm),
   dataType:"jsonp",
   success: function(data){
     //create the pageID by stripping
     //all non-alphanumeric data
     var pageId = searchTerm.replace(/[^a-zA-Z0-9]+/g,"");
     //throw the pageId and original search term
     //into the data that we'll be sending to JSRenderdata.pageId =
pageId;
     data.searchTerm = searchTerm;

     //render the page and append it to the document body
$(document.body).append($("#twitterSearchPageTemplate")
       .render(data));

     //set the page to remove itself once left
     $("#"+pageId).attr( "data-" + $.mobile.ns
       + "external-page", true )
       .one( 'pagecreate', $.mobile._bindPageRemove );
     //switch to the new page
     $.mobile.changePage("#"+data.pageId);
   }
 })
 .error(function(jqXHR, textStatus, errorThrown){
   //If anything goes wrong, at least we'll know.
   alert(textStatus+" - "+errorThrown);
 });
});
```

First, we pull the search term from the attribute on the link itself. The search term itself is somewhat inappropriate as an `id` attribute for dynamically rendered pages; so, we'll strip out any spaces and non-alphanumeric content. We then append the `pageId` and `searchTerm` attribute to the JSON object we received back from Twitter. Following is a sample of returned data from this call:

```
jQuery1720026425381423905492_1345774796765({
    "completed_in": 0.02,
    "max_id": 238829616129777665,
    "max_id_str": "238829616129777665",
```

```json
    "next_page": "?page=2&max_id=238829616129777665&q=%23ThingsISay
TooMuch",
    "page": 1,
    "query": "%23ThingsISayToMuch",
    "refresh_url": "?since_id=238829616129777665&q=%23ThingsISay
TooMuch",
    "results": [
        {
            "created_at": "Fri, 24 Aug 2012 02:46:24 +0000",
            "from_user": "MichelleEspra",
            "from_user_id": 183194730,
            "from_user_id_str": "183194730",
            "from_user_name": "Michelle Espranita",
            "geo": null,
            "id": 238829583808483328,
            "id_str": "238829583808483328",
            "iso_language_code": "en",
            "metadata": {
                "result_type": "recent"
            },
            "profile_image_url": "http:\/\/a0.twimg.com\/profile_
images\/2315127236\/Photo_20on_202012-03-03_20at_2001.39_20_232_
normal.jpg",
            "profile_image_url_https": "https:\/\/si0.
twimg.com\/profile_images\/2315127236\/Photo_20on_202012-03-
03_20at_2001.39_20_232_normal.jpg",
            "source": "&lt;a href=&quot;http:\/\/twitter.
com\/&quot;&gt;web&lt;\/a&gt;",
            "text": "RT @MuchOfficial: @MichelleEspra I'd be the
aforementioned Much! #ThingsISayTooMuch",
            "to_user": null,
            "to_user_id": 0,
            "to_user_id_str": "0",
            "to_user_name": null,
            "in_reply_to_status_id": 238518389595840512,
            "in_reply_to_status_id_str": "238518389595840512"
        }

    }
```

So, we'll take this response and pass it into the renderer to be transformed against twitterSearchPageTemplate:

```html
<script id="twitterSearchPageTemplate" type="text/x-jsrender">
    <div id="{{>pageId}}" data-role="page" data-add-back-btn="true">
        <div data-role="header">
            <h1>{{>searchTerm}}</h1>
```

```
    </div>
    <div data-role="content">
      <ul id="results" data-role="listview" data-dividertheme="b">
        {{for results}}
          <li class="twitterItem">
          <a href="http://twitter.com/{{>from_user}}">
            <img src="{{>profile_image_url}}" alt="{{>from_user_
name}}" class="ui-shadow ui-corner-all" />
              <h3>{{>from_user_name}}</h3>
                <span class="handle">
                  (@{{>from_user}})<br/>
                  {{>location}}
                    {{if geo}}
                      {{>geo}}
                    {{/if}}
                </span>
              </h3>
              <p>{{>text}}</p>
          </a>
        </li>
        {{/for}}
      </ul>
    </div>
  </div>
</script>
```

These are simple implementations. The examples on GitHub show many more options that are worth exploring. Check out `http://borismoore.github.com/jsrender/demos/` for details on creating more complex templates. This is a rapidly changing library (most client-side templating libraries are). So don't be surprised if, by the time you read this, there are a lot more options and slightly changed syntax.

Once we have the results of the transformation, we'll be ready to append the new page's source to the document's body and then programmatically change to this new page.

Programmatically changing pages

There are two ways to programmatically change pages in jQuery Mobile, and the differences are subtle:

- Call `$.mobile.changePage` and pass in a selector to the ID of the page you want to go to. This works the same way with URLs. Either way will yield the same results as if the user had clicked on a link. The page is inserted into the browser's history as one might expect. Following is the example code:

  ```
  $.mobile.changePage("#"+data.pageId);
  ```

- Create a jQuery object by selecting the page you want to change to first. Then, pass that jQuery object into the `$.mobile.changePage` function. The result is that the page is shown but the URL never updates, and, thus, it does not exist in the browser's history. This might be useful in situations where, if the user refreshes the page, you would want them to start the process over at the first screen. It prevents deep linking through bookmarks into other pages in a multipage layout. Following is an example:

  ```
  var $newPage = $("#"+data.pageId);
  $.mobile.changePage($newPage);
  ```

Generated pages and DOM weight management

In the normal course of events while surfing traditional mobile sites, jQuery Mobile will mark each page as `external-page`, which will cause the page to be removed from the DOM once the user navigates away from that page. The idea behind this is that it will manage DOM weight because "budget" (crappy) devices may not have as much memory to dedicate to their browsers. External pages will likely still be in the device cache for quick recall. So reloading them should be lightning fast. If you want to learn more about how jQuery Mobile handles this behavior, check out `http://jquerymobile.com/demos/1.3.0/docs/pages/page-cache.html`.

jQuery Mobile has done a great job at managing DOM weight through normal means. However, when we dynamically create pages, they are not automatically deleted from the DOM on exit. This can become especially overwhelming if there are a lot of them. We could easily overwhelm the miserable browsers on dumb phones and even some of the early-model or budget smartphones. If a dynamically-created page is likely to be viewed again within a session, then it may well be worth leaving in the DOM. However, since we're generating it in the browser to begin with, it's probably safer and faster to just re-render the page.

You can mark a page for deletion using this line of code *after* the page has been rendered but *before* the page is initialized:

```
$("#"+pageId).attr( "data-" + $.mobile.ns + "external-page", true
).one( 'pagecreate', $.mobile._bindPageRemove );
```

WARNING: This line of code comes almost verbatim from the library code itself. This is how they do it behind the scenes. Please note that `$.mobile._bindPageRemove` begins with an underscore. We are not dealing with a public method here.

This particular code is an undocumented and unofficial part of the API, which means that it could be changed on any given release. As central as this is to the framework, I doubt they'll change it; however, anytime you start introducing code that relies on continued presence of non-public APIs, you run the risk of an upgrade breaking your code without any warning in the release notes. Use freely, but thoroughly test each library upgrade.

Leveraging RSS feeds

What can I say? My editors made me do it. I hadn't initially planned on building anything around RSS. I'm glad they did because after looking around, there's a lot more information out there being fed by RSS than by JSON feeds. I figured the digital world had advanced a little more than it really had. So, Usha, thank you for making me include this.

First things first, if we don't use a server-side proxy, we will crash right into the unforgiving wall of the same-original policy. Examples include cURL in PHP systems, Apache HTTP Core Components in Java, or something like HttpWebRequest on .Net.

Following is the page I created in PHP to leverage cURL to grab the Ars Technica feed. The source for this file is in `ars.php` in the chapter code bundle.

```
<?PHP

//based on original example from...
//http://www.jonasjohn.de/snippets/php/curl-example.htm

//is cURL installed yet?
if (!function_exists('curl_init')){
  die('Sorry cURL is not installed!');
}
```

```
// OK cool. Then, let's create a new cURL resource handle
$ch = curl_init();

// Now set some options (most are optional)
// Set URL to download
curl_setopt($ch, CURLOPT_URL, "http://feeds.arstechnica.com/
arstechnica/index?format=xml");

// Set a referer
curl_setopt($ch, CURLOPT_REFERER, "http://bookexample/chapter5");

// User agent
curl_setopt($ch, CURLOPT_USERAGENT, "BookExampleCurl/1.0");

// Include header in result? (0 = yes, 1 = no)
curl_setopt($ch, CURLOPT_HEADER, 0);

// Should cURL return or print out the data?
// (true = return, false = print)
curl_setopt($ch, CURLOPT_RETURNTRANSFER, true);

// Timeout in seconds
curl_setopt($ch, CURLOPT_TIMEOUT, 10);

// Download the given URL, and return output
$output = curl_exec($ch);

// Close the cURL resource, and free system resources curl_close($ch);

echo $output;
?>
```

WARNING: cURL and other server-side proxy libraries are very powerful and, thus, very dangerous tools. Do *not* parameterize the URL that you intend to hit with this page. Hard code the URL. If you must take a parameter from the calling URL to build your destination, then *you must escape all parameters*. If you do not, you can rest assured that someday a hacker is going to have a lot of fun with your site with cross-site scripting (https://www.owasp.org/index.php/Cross-site_Scripting_(XSS)).

Next, let's add some buttons to the top. One for our Twitter feed, and one for Ars Technica. The final source for this next part will be in the file index.html in the code bundle for the chapter:

```
<div data-role="header">
  <h1>News</h1>
</div>
<div data-role="footer">
  <div data-role="navbar">
    <ul>
      <li><a id="twitter" href="#" class="ui-btn-active">Twitter</a></li>
      <li><a id="ars" href="#">Feed</a></li>
    </ul>
  </div>
</div>
<div data-role="content">
  <ul id="results" data-role="listview" data-dividertheme="b"></ul>
</div>
```

Next, let's add to our scripts to load the feed:

```
function loadArs(){
  //scroll back up to the top
  $.mobile.silentScroll(0);

  //Go get the Ars Technica feed content
  $.ajax({
    url:"ars.php",
    dataType:"xml",
    success: function(data, textStatus, jqXHR) {

      //Store the response for later use
      localStorage.setItem("ars", jqXHR.responseText);
      //prepare the content for use
      var $feed = $(data);

      //prepare a list divider with the title of the feed.
      var listView = "<li data-role='list-divider'>"+$feed.find("channel>title").text()+"</li>";
      //loop through every feed item and
      //create a listview element.
      $feed.find("channel>item").each(function(index){
        var $item = $(this);
        listView += "<li><a href='javascript://' "
```

```
        +"data-storyIndex='"+index
        +"' class='arsFeed'><h3>"
        +$item.find("title").text()
        +"</h3><p>"+$item.find("pubDate").text()
        +"</p></a></li>";
    });


    //put the new listview in the main display
    $("#results").html(listView);


    //refresh the listview so it looks right
    $("#results").listview("refresh");


   //place hooks on the newly created links
   //so they trigger the display of the
   //story when clicked
    $("#results a.arsFeed").click(function(){


        //get the feed content back out of storage
var arsData = localStorage.getItem("ars");
        //figure out which story was clicked and
        //pull that story's content from the item
var storyIndex = $(this).attr("data-storyIndex");
        var $item =
          $(arsData).find("channel>item:eq("+storyIndex+")");
        //create a new page with the story content
var storyPage = "<div id='ars"+storyIndex+"' "
        +"data-role='page' data-add-back-btn='true'>"
        +"<div data-role='header'><h1>Ars Technica</h1>"
        +"</div><div data-role='content'><h2>"
        +$item.find('title').text()+"</h2>"
        +$item.find('content\\:encoded').html()
        +"</div></div>";


        //append the story page to the body
        $("body").append(storyPage);
        //find all the images in the newly
        //created page.
        $("#ars"+storyIndex+" img").each(function(index, element) {
          var $img = $(element);
          //figure out its currentWidth
          var currentWidth = Number($img.attr("width"));
          //if it has a width and it's large
          if(!isNaN(currentWidth) && currentWidth > 300){
```

```
                //remove the explicit width and height
$img.removeAttr("width").removeAttr("height");
                //make the image scale to the width
//of it's container but never to be
//larger than its original size
                $img.css({"max-width":currentWidth
                   +"px","width":"100%"});
            }
         });

         //switch to the new page
         $.mobile.changePage("#ars"+storyIndex);
      });
   }
 });
}


$("#ars").click(loadArs);
```

Here's what our new feed reader looks like!

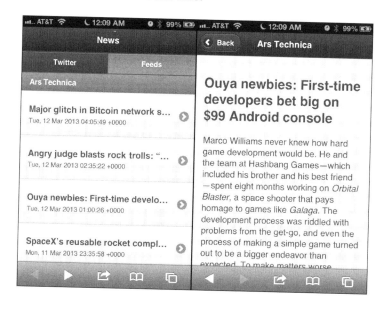

Forcing responsive images

When you're importing from a page where you have no control over the images embedded in the content, you may have to tweak them to get it to look right in mobile. As in the previous example, I've found it's best to remove the explicit width and heights on the image itself and use CSS to make it fill 100 percent of its current container. Then, use a CSS `max-width` property to ensure the image is never scaled beyond it's original intended sizes.

While not truly being responsive in terms of loading a different size of the image that is appropriate for the resolution based on media queries, we've accomplished the same visible effect with the limited resources at our disposal for cases like this.

HTML5 Web Storage

HTML5 Web Storage is ridiculously simple if you haven't messed with it already. If you have, skip to the next paragraph. There are really only two forms of web storage: `localStorage`, and `sessionStorage`. `localStorage` will keep the information indefinitely. `sessionStorage` will store only for the length of a single session. It's a simple key/value paired system. Everything is string-based. So you'll need to convert the values to other formats as needed, once you've extracted them back out of storage. Check out `http://www.w3schools.com/html5/html5_webstorage.asp` for more information.

Now, this gets interesting with the definition of session. *Do not confuse* the session on your server with the browser session. The user session on your server might be set to expire within 20 minutes or so. However, just because your server session has expired, doesn't mean that your browser knows anything about that. *HTML5 session storage will persist until the browser is actually closed.*

This gets especially tricky on mobile browsers. In both Android and iOS, when you switch tasks or press the home button, the browser doesn't actually close. In both cases, you have to actually use the task killer functions to completely close the browsers. This is something that the end user might not actually do on their own.

But what's the big deal about web storage? Why not just use cookies to store information on the client? After all, it will work with everyone, right? Yes, cookies will work for everyone. However, they were never meant to store massive amounts of data like we're using in this example, and there is a soft limit to the number of cookies you can even store per domain (anywhere from 20-50 depending on the browser). The worst part about trying to use cookies for client-side storage is that they are sent back to the server as part of the request *for every single asset served from that domain*. That means that every CSS, JS, image, and page/Ajax request will carry every cookie with its payload. You can see how this could quickly start to degrade your performance. Adding one cookie could result in that data's transmission many times just to render a single page.

Browser-based databases (a work in progress)

Browser-based databases are in a state of extreme flux right now. There are actually two different standards available at the moment. The first is **Web SQL Database** (`http://www.w3.org/TR/webdatabase/`). You could use it, but, according to the W3C, this spec is no longer active. Many browsers have implemented Web SQL Database, but how long will it be around?

The W3C has, instead, stated that the direction for database on the browser will be **Indexed Database** (`http://www.w3.org/TR/IndexedDB/`). The working draft has editors from Microsoft, Google, and Mozilla; so, we can expect broad support in the future. The problem here is that the working draft was published May 24, 2012. As of the time of writing this chapter, only Firefox, Chrome, and Internet Explorer 10 are supporting IndexedDB (`http://en.wikipedia.org/wiki/Indexed_Database_API`).

JSON to the rescue

For now, we find ourselves in a terrible position of either using a doomed database or waiting for everyone to catch up with the new spec. Web Storage looks like the only safe bet in the near future. So, how can we best leverage that? With JSON, of course! All major browsers support JSON natively.

Think about the way we've always had to deal with relational databases in the past. As object-oriented programmers, we've always done our query and then taken the results data and turned it into an object in memory. We can do almost the exact same thing by simply storing JSON directly to a key in Web Storage by using the `JSON.stringify` method.

Here is an example to test if your system natively supports JSON. The source is `jsonTest.html` in the chapter code bundle:

```html
<!DOCTYPE html>
<html>
<head>
  <title>JSON Test</title>
</head>
<body>
<script type="text/javascript">

  var myFeedList = {
    "lastUpdated":"whenever",
    "feeds":[
    {
        "name":"ars",
      "url":"http://feeds.arstechnica.com/arstechnica/
index?format=xml"
      },
      {
        "name":"rbds",
        "url":"http://roughlybrilliant.com/rss.xml"

      }
      ]
    }

  myFeedList.lastUpdated = new Date();

  localStorage.feedList = JSON.stringify(myFeedList);

  var myFeedListRetrieved = JSON.parse(localStorage.feedList);
  alert(myFeedListRetrieved.lastUpdated);
</script>
</body>
</html>
```

If all is well, you'll see an alert containing a timestamp.

If, for some reason, you find yourself in the unlucky position of having to support some massively out-of-date system (Windows Phone 7 and BlackBerry 5 or 6, I'm looking at you), go get `json2.js` from `https://github.com/douglascrockford/JSON-js` and include it with your other scripts. Then, you'll be able to stringify and parse JSON.

Leveraging the Google Feeds API

So, we've seen how to natively pull in a normal RSS feed, parse, and build out the pages using normal, tedious string concatenation. Now, let's consider an alternative that I had no idea even existed when I first started writing this chapter. Thanks go to Raymond Camden and Andy Matthews for pointing this out in their book, *jQuery Mobile Web Development Essentials*. You need to follow those two on Twitter at @cfjedimaster and @commadelimited.

The Google Feeds API can be fed several options, but at its core, it's a way to specify an RSS or ATOM feed and get back a JSON representation. Naturally, this opens up a few more interesting doors in this chapter. If we can now pull in multiple feeds of different types without having to have any kind of server-side proxy, we can greatly simplify our lives. Client-side templates are back in the picture! No more string concatenation! Since they're all in a unified format (including the publish date), we can pull them all together into one master view with all feed stories sorted by date.

Sorting objects by their properties is actually pretty simple. You just have to pass a function to do the comparison. The following code is what we'll use for the date:

```
function compareDates(a,b) {
  var aPubDate = Date.parse(a.publishedDate);
  var bPubDate = Date.parse(b.publishedDate);
  if ( aPubDate < bPubDate) return 1;
  if (aPubDate > bPubDate)  return -1;
  return 0;
}
```

Now, let's specify a JSON object to store the feeds we want to use:

```
var allFeeds = {

  //all the feeds we want to pull in
  "sources":[
"http://feeds.arstechnica.com/arstechnica/index?format=xml",
"http://rss.slashdot.org/Slashdot/slashdot",
"http://www.theregister.co.uk/headlines.atom"
],

  //How many of the feeds have responded?  Once all have
  //responded, we'll finish our processing.
  "sourcesReporting":0,

  //This is where we will store the returned stories.
  "entries":[]
};
```

Next we'll use our processor function to handle the stories as they come in:

```
function assimilateFeed(data){

    //Mark another feed as having reported back
    allFeeds.sourcesReporting++;

    //Grab the title of this feed
    var feedTitle = data.responseData.feed.title;

    //Loop through every entry returned and add the feed title
    //as the source for the story
    for(x = 0; x < data.responseData.feed.entries.length;
        data.responseData.feed.entries[x++].source=feedTitle);

    //Join this field's entries with whatever entries might have
    //already been loaded
    allFeeds.entries = allFeeds.entries.concat(data.responseData.feed.
entries);

    //If all the feeds have reported back, it's time to process
    if(allFeeds.sourcesReporting == allFeeds.sources.length){

        //Sort all the stories by date
        allFeeds.entries.sort(compareDates);

        //Take the results that have now all been combined and
        //sorted by date and use jsRender
        $("#results").html($("#googleFeedTemplate")
            .render(allFeeds)).listview("refresh");

    }
}
```

Here's our JsRender template:

```
<script type="text/x-jsrender" id="googleFeedTemplate">
  {{for entries}}
    <li>
      <a href="{{:link}}" target="_blank">
        <h3>{{:title}}</h3>
        <p><strong>{{:source}}</strong> - {{:publishedDate}}
          <br/>{{:contentSnippet}}
        </p>
      </a>
    </li>
  {{/for}}
</script>
```

And finally, here is the function that will kick off the whole thing:

```javascript
$("#feeds").click( function() {

    //Reset the number of received feeds
    allFeeds.sourcesReporting = 0;

    //Get back to the top of the page
    $.mobile.silentScroll(0);

    //Loop through all the feeds
    for(var x = 0; x < allFeeds.sources.length; x++){
        $.ajax({

//Call to Google's Feed API with the URL encoded
url:"https://ajax.googleapis.com/ajax/services/feed/load?v=1.0&output=
json&q="+escape(allFeeds.sources[x]),
            dataType:"jsonp",
            success:assimilateFeed
        });
    }
});
```

I've included this as part of my functional example in the `challenge.html` file, but the source goes much deeper than that. The source of `challenge.html` has several hidden gems for you to find as well. I tossed in Reddit, Flickr, and a local search of Twitter while I was at it.

Summary

You have been presented with a very wide array of choices for client-side templating. At this point, you now know how to leverage JSON and JSONP and combine them effectively to create pages on the fly. RSS should present no real challenge to you at this point either, since you can do it either natively or using Google Feeds.

In the next chapter, we'll combine some of these techniques as we continue to build our technical tool chest and turn our eyes to HTML5 Audio.

6
HTML5 Audio

Let's take what we've learned so far and turn our eyes to the music scene. We're going to take the jQuery Mobile interface and turn it into a media player, artist showcase, and information hub that can be saved to people's home screens.

In this chapter, we will cover:

- HTML5 Audio (the progressive enhancement way)
- Fixed position, persistent toolbars (really!?)
- Custom JavaScript controls for HTML5 Audio
- HTML5 Audio in iOS and how it is different
- The all-in-one solution (multipage made useful)
- Saving to the home screen with HTML5 manifest

HTML5 Audio

Say hello to Lindsey Stirling. Lindsey burst onto the scene on season five of America's Got Talent. Have you ever seen a violinist *rock out*? Since her appearance on the national stage, she's been lighting up YouTube with millions of views per video. On September 18, 2012, she released her first self-titled album. This chapter will be a fan tribute centering on her music and digital presence. If you want the full experience, go to her YouTube channel `http://youtube.com/lindseystomp`. Her 2 million subscribers can't be wrong!

Now, back to business. As we've seen so far, jQuery Mobile makes everything easy. You almost have to try to make things complicated. HTML5 Audio can be as complicated as you want it to be and we will get there. For now, let's see just how ridiculously simple it can be to bring audio into your jQuery Mobile pages. Consider the following code snippet:

```
<audio id="audio" controls>
  <source src="audio/electricdaisy.mp3" type="audio/mpeg" />
  <source src="audio/electricdaisy.ogg" type="audio/ogg" />
  Your browser is so old that you can't hear the music.
</audio>
```

That's it. That's all it took to get that music control bar in the previous image. Let's break this down just a little.

Just like in the video from *Chapter 4, QR Codes, Geolocation, Google Maps API, and HTML5 Video*, the audio tags can support multiple sources and the browser will simply choose the first one it knows how to deal with. Older browsers won't have a clue what to do and will simply parse this like XML, which means that the only thing that will show up is the text, "Your browser is so old that you can't hear the music."

Each browser provides its own native interface for controlling the audio. Some are tiny and shiny like the iOS version you just saw, and some are completely ugly but more usable such as Android. Regardless, they all leave something to be desired so let's turn jQuery Mobile into a media player.

Here is our base starting page. You can find the source for this in `electricdaisy_basic.html` in the code files:

```html
<!DOCTYPE html>
<html>
  <head>
    <meta charset="utf-8">
    <meta name="viewport" content="width=device-width, initial-scale=1, maximum-scale=1.0, user-scalable=no">
    <link href='chapter6.css' rel='stylesheet' type='text/css'>
    <title>Lindsey Sterling</title>
    <link rel="stylesheet" href="http://code.jquery.com/mobile/1.3.0/jquery.mobile-1.3.0.min.css" />
    <script src="http://code.jquery.com/jquery-1.8.2.min.js"></script>
    <script type="text/javascript" src="js/global.js"></script>
    <script src="http://code.jquery.com/mobile/1.3.0/jquery.mobile-1.3.0.min.js"></script>
    <link rel="stylesheet" href="chapter6.css" />
  </head>
<body>
<div id="electricdaisy" class="songPage" data-role="page" >
  <div data-role="header">
    <a href="basic.html" data-transition="slidedown" data-theme="c" data-icon="home" data-iconpos="notext">Home</a>
    <h2>Lindsey Sterling</h2>
    <a class="ui-btn-right" data-transition="slidedown" data-theme="c" href="tracklist.html" data-icon="note" data-iconpos="notext" >Music</a>
  </div>
  <div data-role="content">
    <img alt="cover art" src="images/electricdaisy.jpg" width="100%" />
    <p>
      <audio id="audio" controls>
        <source src="audio/electricdaisy.mp3" type="audio/mpeg" />
        <source src="audio/electricdaisy.ogg" type="audio/ogg" />
        Your browser is very old so that you can't hear the music.
      </audio>
    </p>
  </div>
</div>
</body>
</html>
```

This well-constructed jQuery Mobile page doesn't need JavaScript for any purpose other than beautification. You can turn off JS and the whole page still works and still plays music. For all those progressive enhancement fans out there, we're starting off on the right foot. After all, everyone is a fan of music, not just people with smartphones.

Now let's see what we can do around creating a better control interface using JavaScript and fixed position toolbars.

Fixed position persistent toolbars (really!?)

I'll be honest; I have a generally low opinion of fixed position toolbars in the mobile space. From a usability standpoint, they're a disaster. Mobile screens have very little usable space to begin with. To waste that much more real estate without providing a *strong* benefit to the user, is unthinkable. Moreover, because of the CSS involved, ancient versions of Android (less than Version 2.3) will not support the fixed position toolbar.

<rant>Yet, we see it all the time don't we? Companies slap their logo on a top toolbar that never goes away. They throw on a little global navigation and call it a benefit to the user when really it's all about them reinforcing their branding. You can tell because the only interactive parts on the bar are a menu button and possibly a search button (as if we couldn't have found them again at the top). There are many better techniques to provide global navigation. </rant>

Today, we have a valid use for these bars. We're going to put music controls in them that will persist as we transition tracks. If we do the job right, this music website will feel more like an app and give the user constant control over the sound coming from their device.

If you've already played with this part of the jQM UI, skip to the next paragraph now.

Making a toolbar fixed (doesn't move as you scroll) and persistent (doesn't move as you change pages) is pretty simple really. All you have to do is add `data-position="fixed"` to make it fixed and give `data-id="whatever"` to the footers on the pages where you want the footer to hold still as the page transitions behind it. This functionality also works with headers.

Here is the basis for our persistent footer:

```
<div class="jsShow playcontrols" data-role="footer" data-
id="playcontrols" data-position="fixed">
  <div class="progressContainer">
    <input  data-theme="b" data-track-theme="c" class="progressBar"
type="range" name="slider-1"  value="0" min="0" max="227" data-
mini="true"/></div>
  <div data-role="navbar" class="playcontrols">
    <ul>
      <li><a data-theme="c" title="skip back" class="skipback"
href="#crystallize" data-direction="reverse"><img src="images/xtras-
gray/sg_skipback2x.png" alt="Skip Back" height="14"/></a></li>
      <li><a data-theme="c" title="seek back" class="seekback"
href="javascript://"><img src="images/xtras-gray/sg_rw@2x.png"
alt="Seek Back" height="14"/></a></li>
      <li><a data-theme="c" title="play/pause" class="play"
href="javascript://"><img src="images/xtras-gray/49-play@2x.png"
alt="Play/Pause" height="14"/></a></li>
      <li><a data-theme="c" title="seek forward" class="seek"
href="javascript://"><img src="images/xtras-gray/sg_ff@2x.png"
alt="Seek Forward" height="14"/></a></li>
      <li><a data-theme="c" title="skip forward" class="skip"
href="#shadows"><img src="images/xtras-gray/sg_skip@2x.png" alt="Skip
Forward" height="14"/></a></li>
      </li>
    </ul>
  </div>
</div>
```

See that class up at the top of the footer (jsShow)? Let's add another class (jsHide) to the paragraph surrounding the audio tag:

```
<p class="jsHide">
  <audio id="audio" controls>
  ...
</p>
```

In the CSS, let's add the following rules:

```
.js .jsHide{display:none}
.no-js .jsShow{display:none;}
```

Then we'll add a line to our global.js file to pull the whole thing together:

```
$("html").removeClass("no-js").addClass("js");
```

This is a technique used by the HTML5 boilerplate (`http://html5boilerplate.com/`) and Modernizer (`http://modernizr.com/`). If you've not looked at these two marvels, it's worth your time. The long and short of it is that we now have a handy, lightweight way of handling progressive enhancement. Voice assist also works perfectly for those who need the assistance.

We're very close now to having a nice universal UI for a media player, but if you've been typing along, you've notice that the input `type="range"` is showing a textbox. On its own this probably wouldn't be too offensive but the fact that HTML5 Audio keeps track of its current position in terms of seconds makes it pretty useless as a display element. So, let's hide it and expand the bar a bit with some simple CSS:

```
input.progressBar{display:none}
div.ui-slider{width:90%;}
```

Now, that we're looking good, let's wire the thing together and make it work.

Controlling HTML5 Audio with JavaScript

Alright then, here we start to get a little bit more hairy with JavaScript.

First, let's set up an interval to update the progress bar. It's going to have to serve two functions, displaying the current time and changing the time. We'll start by adding references to these objects as well as placing event hooks for every one of the audio events that we might want to attach to. The comments describe which events are fired when:

```
//for every song page
$(document).on("pagecreate", ".songPage", function(){
  var $page = $(this);
  var $currentAudio = $page.find("audio");

  //set references to the playing status, progress bar, and
  //progress interval on the audio object itself
  $currentAudio.data("playing",false)
    .data("progressBar", $page.find("input.progressBar")).
data("progressThread",null);

  //loadstart and progress occur with autoload
  $currentAudio[0].addEventListener('loadstart', function(){
    //Fires when the browser starts looking
    //for the audio/video
  }, false);
```

```
$currentAudio[0].addEventListener('progress', function(){
  //Fires when the browser is downloading the audio/video
  //This will fire multiple times until the source
  //is fully loaded.
}, false);

//durationchange, loadedmetadata, loadeddata, canplay,
//canplaythrough are kicked off upon pressing play
$currentAudio[0].addEventListener('durationchange',
function(){
  //Fires when the duration of the audio/video is changed

}, false);

$currentAudio[0].addEventListener('loadedmetadata',
function(){
  //Fires when the browser has loaded meta data
  //for the audio/video

}, false);

$currentAudio[0].addEventListener('loadeddata', function(){
  //Fires when the browser has loaded the current
  //frame of the audio/video

}, false);

$currentAudio[0].addEventListener('canplay', function(){
  //Fires when the browser can start playing
  //the audio/video

}, false);

$currentAudio[0].addEventListener('canplaythrough',
function(){
  //Fires when the browser can play through the audio/video
  //without stopping for buffering

}, false);

$currentAudio[0].addEventListener('ended', function(){
  //Fires when the current playlist is ended

}, false);
```

```
$currentAudio[0].addEventListener('error', function(){
  //Fires when an error occurred during the loading
  //of an audio/video

}, true);

});
```

Now, let's create the function that will run the interval:

```
function scrubberUpdateInterval(){

  //Grab the current page
  var $page = $.mobile.activePage;

  //Grab the audio element
  var $audio = $page.find("audio");
  var currentAudio = $audio[0];

  //Grab the progress monitor and the handle
  currentAudioProgress = $page.find("input.progressBar");
  scrubberHandle = currentAudioProgress
    .closest(".progressContainer")
    .find("a.ui-slider-handle");

  //Is the user currently touching the bar?
  if(scrubberHandle.hasClass("ui-focus")){
    //Pause it if it's not paused already
    if(!currentAudio.paused){
      currentAudio.pause();
    }

    //Find the last scrubber's last position
    var lastScrubPosition = currentAudioProgress
      .data("lastScrubPosition");
    if(lastScrubPosition == null) lastScrubPosition = 0;
    //Are we in the same place as we were last?
    if(Math.floor(lastScrubPosition) ==
    Math.floor(currentAudio.currentTime)){
      var lastScrubUnchangedCount = currentAudioProgress
        .data("lastScrubUnchangedCount");
      //If the user held still for 3 or more cycles of the
      //interval, resume playing
      if(++lastScrubUnchangedCount >= 2){
```

```
        scrubberHandle.removeClass("ui-focus");
        currentAudioProgress
          .data("lastScrubUnchangedCount", 0);
        currentAudio.play();
      }else{
        //increment the unchanged counter
        currentAudioProgress.data("lastScrubUnchangedCount",
        lastScrubUnchangedCount);
      }
    }else{
      //set the unchanged counter to 0 since we're not in the
      //same place
      currentAudioProgress
        .data("lastScrubUnchangedCount", 0);
    }


    //set the last scrubbed position on the scrubber
    currentAudioProgress.data("lastScrubPosition",
      Number(currentAudioProgress.val()));
    //set the current time of the audio
    currentAudio.currentTime = currentAudioProgress.val();
  }else{
    //The user is not touching the scrubber, just update the
    //position of the handle
    currentAudioProgress
      .val(currentAudio.currentTime)
      .slider('refresh');
  }
}
}
```

Now we'll just kick off the interval when the play button is clicked and do the other necessary things. As usual, everything is well commented:

```
$(document).on('vclick', "a.play", function(){
  try{
    var $page = $.mobile.activePage;
    var $audio = $page.find("audio");

    //toggle playing
    $audio.data("playing",!$audio.data("playing"));
    //if we should now be playing
    if($audio.data("playing")) {

      //play the audio
      $audio[0].play();
```

```
        //switch the playing image for pause
        $page.find("img.playPauseImage")
          .attr("src","images/xtras-gray/48-pause@2x.png");
        //kick off the progress interval
        $audio.data("progressThread",
          setInterval(scrubberUpdateInterval, 750));
      }else{
        //pause the audio
        $audio[0].pause();

        //switch the pause image for the playing audio
    $page.find("img.playPauseImage")
          .attr("src","images/xtras-gray/49-play@2x.png");
        //stop the progress interval
        clearInterval($audio.data("progressThread"));

      }
    }catch(e){alert(e)};
  });
```

Setting seek controls:

```
$(document).on('click', "a.seekback", function(){
  $.mobile.activePage.find("audio")[0].currentTime -= 5.0;
});


$(document).on('vclick', "a.seek", function(){
  $.mobile.activePage.find("audio")[0].currentTime += 5.0;
});
```

Now, let's create a JSON object to track our current state and track list:

```
var media = {
  "currentTrack":0,
  "random":false,
  "tracklist":[
    "electricdaisy.html",
    "comewithus.html",
    "crystallize.html",
    "shadows.html",
    "skyrim.html"
  ]
}
```

Next up, the skip back and forward buttons. We could set up the random button but for now we'll skip that:

```
$(document).on('vclick', "a.skipback", function(event){
  //grab the current audio
  var currentAudio = $.mobile.activePage.find("audio")[0];
  //if we're more than 5 seconds into the song, skip back to
  //the beginning
  if(currentAudio.currentTime > 5){
    currentAudio.currentTime = 0;
  }else{
    //otherwise, change to the previous track
    media.currentTrack--;
    if(media.currentTrack < 0) media.currentTrack =
      (media.tracklist.length - 1);
    $.mobile.changePage("#"+media.tracklist[currentTrack]);
  }
});


$(document).on("vclick", "a.skip", function(event){
  //grab the current audio and switch to the next track
  var currentAudio = $.mobile.activePage.find("audio")[0];
  media.currentTrack++;
  if(media.currentTrack >= media.tracklist.length)
  media.currentTrack = 0;
  $.mobile.changePage("#"+media.tracklist[currentTrack]);
});
```

Performance Note

Notice how I've have shifted away from using the `click` event and I'm now using the `vclick` event. The `vclick` event is a custom event in jQuery Mobile that attempts to bridge the performance gap between click (a desktop-based event) and tap/touchstart (touch-based events). There is generally about a 300-millisecond gap between the two and which browser supports what is always a hard thing to figure out. By using `vclick` you can still support desktop and touch devices but you can hopefully realize a slight performance boost. For more about this, check out the blog post by one of the jQuery Mobile contributors, John Bender at `https://coderwall.com/p/bdxjzg`.

HTML5 Audio in iOS is different

Understanding the event cycle of HTML5 Audio is critical to making it work right. This can get especially confusing when you start mixing in the odd event cycles of jQuery Mobile. Add to that a confusing set of resource restrictions that differ per device and you've got a real recipe for confusion.

As a quick and easy way of testing mobile sites, you can usually just open up Google Chrome (since its WebKit) or IE9 (for the Windows Phone) and shrink it down to mobile size. Naturally, this does not substitute for real testing. Always check your creations on real devices. That being said, the shrunken browser approach will usually get you 97.5 percent of the way there. Well... HTML5 Audio throws that operating model right out the window.

On iOS, even if you've tagged the `audio` tag to preload and autoplay, it won't. No error is thrown; no indication is given that your coded requests were completely ignored. If you look at the code included for this chapter, you'll see in the `basicPlayer.js` script how many try/catch and debug statements I've put in while trying to make this work, and figure out what was going wrong.

Technically, `pageinit` is the event that the documentation says is equivalent to `document.ready` but that doesn't mean that the page is actually visible yet. The end of the event chain leading to page reveal is the `pageshow` event. So, no matter what, that should be the end and it should be ready for whatever you might want to do. At this time, you should (theoretically) be able to tell the song to play (`.play()`) using JavaScript. Alas, it just doesn't work this way. You can take the exact same function used to trigger the audio play from pressing the play button and even kick it off with a time delay and yet nothing works. It's not a timing issue. iOS requires direct user interaction to kick off the audio for the first time. *Tie it directly to the click event or it won't work.*

The all-in-one solution (multipage made useful)

We now have a full-blown player with a unified interface that could be used to manage a playlist. The only real problem we have at this point is network latency. Even in this new age of 4G and LTE, cellular latency can get ridiculous. This is especially true if you work at a place like I do where the building pushes back signals like a Spartan phalanx. So, in order to give this an even better user experience, we're going to abandon this page-by-page business.

While we're at it, let's pack in some of what we've done in previous chapters such as bringing in Lindsey's latest tweet and the content from her blog. We'll use the same CSS from before but we'll change the rest.

One of the first things that starts to annoy server-side and object-oriented types is how often you have to repeat a chunk of code. This becomes a real issue if there is a global header or footer. So, let's create a `div` tag to house the universal footer content and a script to pull it in at the right time:

```
<div id="universalPlayerControls" style="display:none">
  <div class="progressContainer">
    <input  data-theme="b" data-track-theme="c" class="progressBar"
type="range" name="slider-1"  value="0" min="0" max="227" data-
mini="true"/>
  </div>
  <div data-role="navbar" class="playcontrols">
    <ul>
      <li><a data-theme="c" title="skip back" class="skipback"
href="javascript://" data-direction="reverse"><img src="images/xtras-
gray/sg_skipback2x.png" alt="Skip Back" height="14"/></a></li>
      <li><a data-theme="c" title="seek back" class="seekback"
href="javascript://"><img src="images/xtras-gray/sg_rw@2x.png"
alt="Seek Back" height="14"/></a></li>
      <li><a data-theme="c" title="play/pause" class="play"
href="javascript://"><img class="playPauseImage" src="images/xtras-
gray/49-play@2x.png" alt="Play/Pause" height="14"/></a></li>
      <li><a data-theme="c" title="seek forward" class="seek"
href="javascript://"><img src="images/xtras-gray/sg_ff@2x.png"
alt="Seek Forward" height="14"/></a></li>
      <li><a data-theme="c" title="skip forward" class="skip"
href="javascript://"><img src="images/xtras-gray/sg_skip@2x.png"
alt="Skip Forward" height="14"/></a></li>
    </ul>
  </div>
</div>
```

Now on any page load that wants to have these controls in the footer, we'll just copy this content right into the footer before the page is marked up by jQM:

```
$(document).on("pagebeforecreate", function(){
  $(this).find("div[data-id='playcontrols']")
    .html($("#universalPlayerControls").html());
});
```

Finally, it's time to take every song page and make it dynamic. We remove the individual audio elements and simply link to them in data attributes of the "page". The footer is gone and in its place is empty footer ready for the injection of the controls:

```
<div id="electricdaisy" class="songPage" data-role="page" data-
mp3="audio/electricdaisy.mp3" data-ogg="audio/electricdaisy.ogg">
  <div data-role="header">
    <a href="#home" data-theme="c" data-icon="home" data-
iconpos="notext">Home</a>
    <h2>Electric Daisy</h2>
    <a class="ui-btn-right" data-theme="c" href="#tracklist" data-
icon="note" data-iconpos="notext" >Music</a>
  </div>
  <div data-role="content">
    <img src="images/electricdaisy.jpg" width="100%" />
  </div>
  <div data-role="footer" data-id="playcontrols" data-
position="fixed"></div>
</div>
```

All this will require us to revamp our JavaScript. Some of the pieces will remain the same but since we're down to a single audio element, the code can be simplified. Here is the final source code for the all-in-one version that is in the index.html file of the code bundle available at the Packt Publishing website:

```
<!DOCTYPE html>
<html>
<head>
  <meta charset="utf-8">
  <meta name="viewport" content="width=device-width, initial-scale=1,
maximum-scale=1.0, user-scalable=no">
  <link href='http://fonts.googleapis.com/css?family=Playball'
rel='stylesheet' type='text/css'>
  <title>Lindsey Stirling</title>
  <link rel="stylesheet" href="jquery.mobile-1.2.0-rc.1.min.css" />
  <script src="js/jquery-1.7.2.min.js"></script>
  <script type="text/javascript">
    $(document).bind("mobileinit", function(){
      $.mobile.defaultPageTransition = "slide";
    });
```

```
    </script>
    <script src="js/jquery.mobile-1.2.0-rc.1.min.js"></script>
    <script type="text/javascript"
src="js/jsrender.min.js"></script>
    <link rel="stylesheet" href="chapter6.css" />
</head>
<body id="body">
```

With all the usual stuff out of the way, here is the first "page" of the experience:

```
    <div id="home" data-role="page"
      data-mp3="audio/electricdaisy.mp3"
      data-ogg="audio/electricdaisy.ogg">

      <div data-role="header">
        <h1>Lindsey Stirling</h1>
        <a class="ui-btn-right" data-theme="c" href="#tracklist" data-
icon="note" data-iconpos="notext" >Music</a>
      </div>

      <div data-role="content">
        <ul id="homemenu" data-role="listview" data-inset="true">
          <li><a href="#news">News</a></li>
          <li><a href="#tour">Tour</a></li>
          <li><a href="#comewithus">Music</a></li>
        </ul>
        <div id="twitterFeed">
          <ul class="curl"></ul>
        </div>
      </div>

      <div data-role="footer" data-id="playcontrols" data-
position="fixed">
      </div>

    </div>

    <div data-role="page" id="news">
      <div data-role="header">
        <a href="#home" data-theme="c" data-icon="home" data-
iconpos="notext">Home</a>
        <h2>News/Blog</h2>
      </div>

      <div data-role="content"></div>
    </div>
```

The following page lists all the tracks available to preview:

```
<div id="tracklist" data-role="page">
  <div data-role="header">
    <a href="#home" data-theme="c" data-icon="home" data-
iconpos="notext">Home</a>
    <h2>Track List</h2>
  </div>


    <img src="images/lindsey-header-new1.jpeg"  width="100%"
alt="signature banner" />


  <div data-role="content">
    <ul data-role="listview">
      <li><a class="trackListLink" href="#electricdaisy">Electric
Daisy</a></li>
        <li><a class="trackListLink" href="#shadows">Shadows</a></li>
        <li><a class="trackListLink" href="#comewithus">Come With Us
feat. CSWS</a></li>
        <li><a class="trackListLink" href="#skyrim">Skyrim</a></li>
        <li><a class="trackListLink" href="#crystallize">Crystalli
ze</a></li>
    </ul>
  </div>
</div>
```

Here are the individual song pages. I have not included every song page because that would just be a waste of pages. You'll get the idea of how this works. Note that each page has footer with the same `data-id` attribute. The following allows for the footer to remain in place as pages transition between songs:

```
<div id="shadows" class="songPage" data-role="page"
  data-mp3="audio/shadows.mp3"
  data-ogg="audio/shadows.ogg" >
  <div data-role="header">
    <a href="#home" data-theme="c" data-icon="home" data-
iconpos="notext">Home</a>
    <h2>Shadows</h2>
    <a class="ui-btn-right" data-theme="c" href="#tracklist" data-
icon="note" data-iconpos="notext" >Music</a>
  </div>


  <div data-role="content">
    <img src="images/shadows.jpg" width="100%" alt="cover art" />
  </div>
```

```
    <div data-role="footer" data-id="playcontrols" data-
position="fixed"></div>
  </div>

  <div id="crystallize" class="songPage" data-role="page"
    data-mp3="audio/crystallize.mp3"
    data-ogg="audio/crystallize.ogg">
    <div data-role="header">
      <a href="#home" data-theme="c" data-icon="home" data-
iconpos="notext">Home</a>
      <h2>Crystallize</h2>
      <a class="ui-btn-right" data-theme="c" href="#tracklist" data-
icon="note" data-iconpos="notext" >Music</a>
    </div>

    <div data-role="content">
      <img src="images/crystallize.jpg" width="100%" alt="cover art"
/>
    </div>

    <div data-role="footer" data-id="playcontrols" data-
position="fixed"></div>
  </div>

  <div id="electricdaisy" class="songPage" data-role="page"
    data-mp3="audio/electricdaisy.mp3"
    data-ogg="audio/electricdaisy.ogg">
    <div data-role="header">
      <a href="#home" data-theme="c" data-icon="home" data-
iconpos="notext">Home</a>
      <h2>Electric Daisy</h2>
      <a class="ui-btn-right" data-theme="c" href="#tracklist" data-
icon="note" data-iconpos="notext" >Music</a>
    </div>

    <div data-role="content">
      <img src="images/electricdaisy.jpg" width="100%" alt="cover art"
/>
    </div>

    <div data-role="footer" data-id="playcontrols" data-
position="fixed"></div>
  </div>
```

This part is not a page. It's the hidden master controls that will be imported into each page that plays songs:

```html
<div id="universalPlayerControls" style="display:none">
  <div class="progressContainer">
    <input  data-theme="b" data-track-theme="c" class="progressBar"
type="range" name="slider-1"  value="0" min="0" max="227" data-
mini="true"/>
  </div>
  <div data-role="navbar" class="playcontrols">
    <ul>
      <li><a data-theme="c" title="skip back" class="skipback"
href="javascript://" data-direction="reverse"><img src="images/xtras-
gray/sg_skipback2x.png" alt="Skip Back" height="14"/></a></li>
      <li><a data-theme="c" title="seek back" class="seekback"
href="javascript://"><img src="images/xtras-gray/sg_rw@2x.png"
alt="Seek Back" height="14"/></a></li>
      <li><a data-theme="c" title="play/pause" class="play"
href="javascript://"><img class="playPauseImage" src="images/xtras-
gray/49-play@2x.png" alt="Play/Pause" height="14"/></a></li>
      <li><a data-theme="c" title="seek forward" class="seek"
href="javascript://"><img src="images/xtras-gray/sg_ff@2x.png"
alt="Seek Forward" height="14"/></a></li>
      <li><a data-theme="c" title="skip forward" class="skip"
href="javascript://"><img src="images/xtras-gray/sg_skip@2x.png"
alt="Skip Forward" height="14"/></a></li>
    </ul>
  </div>
</div>

<div style="display:none;">
  <audio id="audio" controls></audio>
</div>
```

The following code is the template for rendering the imported blog content:

```html
<script type="text/x-jsrender" id="googleFeedTemplate">
  <ul class="curl">
    {{for entries}}
      <li>
        <h3 class="ul-li-heading">{{:title}}</h3>
        <p>{{:publishedDate}}<br>{{:content}}</p>
      </li>
    {{/for}}
  </ul>
</script>
```

The following code is the template for rendering the Twitter feed:

```
<script type="text/x-jsrender" id="twitterTemplate">
  <li class="twitterItem">
    <img src="{{:user.profile_image_url}}" alt="profile image"
class="ui-shadow ui-corner-all" />
    <p>{{:text}}</p>
  </li>
</script>

<script type="text/javascript">
  var media = {
    "playing":false,
    "debug":true,
    "currentTrack":0,
    "random":false,
    "tracklist":[
      "#electricdaisy",
      "#comewithus",
      "#crystallize",
      "#shadows",
      "#skyrim"
    ]
  }

  //a handy little debug function
  var lastDebugTS = (new Date).getTime();
  function debug(str){
  try{
      if(media.debug){
        $.mobile.activePage.find("div[data-role='content']")
          .append(""+((new Date()).getTime()-lastDebugTS)+":
"+str+"<br/>");
        lastDebugTS = (new Date).getTime();}
    }catch(e){}
  }

  //grab the audio and control elements with global
  //variables since everything is going to use them
  var currentAudio = $("#audio")[0];
  var currentAudioProgress = null;
  var scrubberHandle = null;
  var scrubberUpdateSpeed = 750;
  var progressThread = null;
```

```
    //The ended and durationchange are the only events we
    //really care about
    currentAudio.addEventListener('ended',
      function(){
        $.mobile.activePage.find(".skip").click()
      }, false); currentAudio.addEventListener('durationchange',
      function(){
        currentAudioProgress.attr('max',currentAudio.duration)
          .slider("refresh");
      });


  //On the home page
  $("#home").live('pagebeforeshow', function(){
    var $page = $(this);


    //bring in the latest tweet
$.ajax({url:"http://api.twitter.com/1/statuses/user_timeline.
json?screen_name="+escape("LindseyStirling"),
      dataType:"jsonp",
      success: function(data) {
        try{
          //parse out any hyperlinks and twitter IDs and turn
          //them into links
          var words = data[0].text.split(" ");
          var newMessage = "";
          for(var x = 0; x < words.length; x++){
          var word = words[x];
            if(word.indexOf("http") == 0){
              newMessage += "<a href='"+word+"' target='_
blank'>"+word+"</a>";
            }else if(word.match(/@[a-zA-Z0-9_]*/)){
      newMessage += "<a href='http://twitter.com/"+word.
substring(1)+"' target='_blank'>"+word+"</a> ";
            }else{
              newMessage += word+" ";
            }
          }
          data[0].text = newMessage;
        }catch(e){}

        //use jsRender to display the message
        $("#twitterFeed ul")
          .html($("#twitterTemplate")
          .render(data[0]));
    }
  });
```

```
    //if we're not currently playing anything, preload audio
    //as specified by the page's data- attributes
    if(!media.playing) {

       //load MP3 by default
       if(currentAudio.canPlayType("audio/mpeg")){
          currentAudio.src = $page.attr("data-mp3");
       }

       //load Ogg for all those purists out there
       else{ currentAudio.src = $page.attr("data-ogg");}
       //make it load
       currentAudio.load();

       //set the progres bar
       currentAudioProgress = $page.find("input.progressBar");
       //set the scrubber handle
       scrubberHandle = currentAudioProgress
          .closest(".progressContainer")
          .find("a.ui-slider-handle");
    }
  });


  //on the news page
  $("#news").live('pageshow', function(){
     //This import can take a while, show the loading message
  $.mobile.loading( 'show', {
       text: "Loading Blog Content",
       textVisible: true
     });

     //load the actual content
     $.ajax({
  url:"https://ajax.googleapis.com/ajax/services/feed/load?v=1.0&outpu
t=json&q="+escape("http://lindseystirlingviolin.com/feed"),
        dataType:"jsonp",
        success: function(data) {
          //use a jsRender template to format the blog
          $("#news .ui-content")
             .html($("#googleFeedTemplate")
             .render(data.responseData.feed));
          //for every image in the news feed, make its width
          //dynamic with a max width or its original size
          $("#news img").each(function(index, element) {
           var $img = $(element);
```

```
                //figure out its currentWidth
                var currentWidth = Number($img.attr("width"));
                //if it has a width and it's large
                if(!isNaN(currentWidth) && currentWidth > 300){
                    //remove the explicit width and height
            $img.removeAttr("width").removeAttr("height");
                    //make the image scale to the width
                //of its container but never to be
                //larger than its original size
                    $img.css({"max-width":currentWidth+"px","width":"100%"});
                }
            });


            //hide the loading
            $.mobile.loading("hide");
        }
    });
});


    function setCurrentMediaSources(){
        var $page = $.mobile.activePage;

        //set the audio to whatever is playable
        var playableSource = $page.attr("data-mp3");
        if(!currentAudio.canPlayType("audio/mpeg")){
            playableSource = $page.attr("data-ogg");
        }
        //set the progress bar and scrubber handles
        currentAudioProgress = $page.find("input.progressBar");
    scrubberHandle = currentAudioProgress
            .closest(".progressContainer")
            .find("a.ui-slider-handle");


        //change the source and load it.
        currentAudio.src = playableSource;
        currentAudio.load();


        //if we're currently play, continue playing
        if(media.playing){
            currentAudio.play();
            progressThread = setInterval(scrubberUpdateThread,
    scrubberUpdateSpeed);
        }
    }
```

```
$(".songPage").live("pageshow", setCurrentMediaSources);

$("[data-role='page']").live("pagebeforecreate",
function(){
  $(this).find("div[data-id='playcontrols']")
    .html($("#universalPlayerControls").html());
});

function scrubberUpdateThread(){
  //if the scrubber has focus, the scrubber becomes
  //input instead of status display
  if(scrubberHandle.hasClass("ui-focus")){

    //pause the music for now
    if(!currentAudio.paused){
      currentAudio.pause();
    }

    //grab the last position to see if we've moved
    var lastScrubPosition =
      currentAudioProgress.data("lastScrubPosition");
    if(lastScrubPosition == null) lastScrubPosition = 0;
    //if the user hasn't scrubbed
    if(Math.floor(lastScrubPosition) == Math.floor(currentAudio.
currentTime)){
      var lastScrubUnchangedCount =
      currentAudioProgress.data("lastScrubUnchangedCount");
      if(++lastScrubUnchangedCount >= 2){
  //since it's been 3 cycles that we haven't moved,
      //remove the focus and play
      scrubberHandle.removeClass("ui-focus");
      currentAudioProgress.data("lastScrubUnchangedCount", 0);
      currentAudio.play();
    }else{

      //store the the current position counter
      currentAudioProgress.data("lastScrubUnchangedCount",
lastScrubUnchangedCount);
    }
    }else{
      //reset the current position counter
      currentAudioProgress.data("lastScrubUnchangedCount", 0);
    }
```

```
      //set the position of the scrubber and the currentTime
      //position of the song itself
      currentAudioProgress.data("lastScrubPosition",
        Number(currentAudioProgress.val()));
      currentAudio.currentTime = currentAudioProgress.val();
    }else{
      //update the progress scrubber
      currentAudioProgress.val(currentAudio.currentTime)
        .slider('refresh');
    }
  }

  //play button controls
  $("a.play").live('click',function(){
    try{
      //toggle the playing status
      media.playing = !media.playing;

      //if we're supposed to playing..
      if(media.playing) {

        //do it and set the interval to watch
        currentAudio.play();
        progressThread = setInterval(scrubberUpdateThread,
scrubberUpdateSpeed);

        //switch the playing image for pause
        $("img.playPauseImage").attr("src","images/xtras-gray/48-
pause@2x.png");
      }else{

        //pause the audio and clear the interval
        currentAudio.pause();

        //switch the pause image for the playing audio
        $("img.playPauseImage").attr("src","images/xtras-gray/49-play@2x.
png");

        //kill the progress interval
        clearInterval(progressThread);
      }
    }catch(e){alert(e)};
  });
```

```
$("a.seekback").live('click',function(){
  //back 5 seconds
  currentAudio.currentTime -= 5.0;
});

$("a.seek").live('click',function(){
  //forward 5 seconds
  currentAudio.currentTime += 5.0;
});

$("a.skipback").live('click',function(event){
  //if we're more than 5 seconds into the song, skip
  //back to the beginning
  if(currentAudio.currentTime > 5){
    currentAudio.currentTime = 0;
  }else{
    //othewise, change to the previous track
    media.currentTrack--;
    if(media.currentTrack < 0) media.currentTrack = (media.tracklist.
length - 1);

    $.mobile.changePage(media.tracklist[media.currentTrack],
    {
        transition: "slide",
        reverse: true
    });
  }
});

$("a.skip").live('click',function(event){
  //pause the audio and reset the time to 0
  currentAudio.currentTime = 0;

  //change to the next track
  media.currentTrack++;
  if(media.currentTrack >= media.tracklist.length) media.currentTrack
= 0;

    $.mobile.changePage(media.tracklist[media.currentTrack]);
});
</script>
</body>
</html>
```

With it all built together into one huge multipage app like this, you will feel the buttery smoothness of the interface. We're using the exact same CSS in this file that we did in the standalone song files.

Saving to the home screen with HTML5 manifest

With great power comes great responsibility. This is a power feature. If you properly leverage the HTML5 manifest and a few other meta tags, your application will become a full-screen, chrome-less app.

To make your apps save down and launch as full-screen apps you'll need icons for your home screen. They'll be squares in sizes of 144, 114, 72, and 57 pixels. Link to them like so:

```
<link rel="apple-touch-icon-precomposed" sizes="144x144" href="images/
album144.png">
<link rel="apple-touch-icon-precomposed" sizes="114x114" href="images/
album114.png">
<link rel="apple-touch-icon-precomposed" sizes="72x72" href="images/
album72.png">
<link rel="apple-touch-icon-precomposed" href="images/album57.png">
<link rel="shortcut icon" href="img/images/album144.png">
```

The user's navigation buttons can be made to disappear on iOS. Be aware that if you choose to do this, you need to provide full navigation within your app. This means you'll probably want to add either a back button. If you want to make the app go full screen, use these tags:

```
<meta name="apple-mobile-web-app-capable" content="yes">
<meta name="apple-mobile-web-app-status-bar-style" content="black">
```

To make the thing available in the offline mode, we'll use the manifest. Manifest uses the application cache to store the assets. There is a limit to how much you can store. This differs from device to device but it's probably less than 25 MB. List what you want saved in the order of priority just to be saved. For a complete breakdown of what all the manifest can do, check out `http://www.html5rocks.com/en/tutorials/appcache/beginner/`.

Here are the contents of our manifest. It is saved under `app.manifest`:

```
CACHE MANIFEST
# 2012-09-21:v1
js/jquery-1.7.2.min.js
js/jquery.mobile-1.2.0-rc.1.min.js
js/global.js
js/jsrender.min.js

audio/shadows.mp3
audio/comewithus.mp3
audio/skyrim.mp3
audio/electricdaisy.mp3
audio/crystallize.mp3

jquery.mobile-1.2.0-rc.1.min.css
chapter6.css

images/xtras-gray/sg_skip.png
images/xtras-gray/sg_skip@2x.png
images/xtras-gray/sg_skipback.png
images/xtras-gray/sg_skipback@2x.png
images/xtras-gray/sg_ff.png
images/xtras-gray/sg_ff@2x.png
images/xtras-gray/sg_rw.png
images/xtras-gray/sg_rw@2x.png
images/xtras-gray/48-pause.png
images/xtras-gray/48-pause@2x.png
images/xtras-gray/49-play.png
images/xtras-gray/49-play@2x.png
images/ajax-loader.gif
images/comewithus.jpg
images/crystallize.jpg
images/electricdaisy.jpg
images/shadows.jpg
images/skyrim.jpg
images/wallpaper.jpg
```

```
images/cork.jpeg
images/icons-18-black.png
images/icons-18-white.png
images/icons-36-black.png
images/icons-36-white.png
images/note18.png
images/note36.png
```

To use the manifest file, your web server or .htaccess will have to be configured to return the type of text/cache-manifest. In the HTML file, all you have to do is add it as an attribute to the html tag itself, like so:

```
<html manifest="app.manifest">
```

If you want to clear your cache, you can always do it through your browser settings. You can also control the cache with JavaScript. The earlier article I linked to provides plenty of detail if you really want to dig in.

Summary

This was a meaty chapter despite its simplistic start. But, you now know pretty much everything there is to know about combining HTML5 Audio with jQuery Mobile. You can create the wonderful academic, progressively enhanced pages and even make complex apps to be saved to devices. If this chapter didn't scare you off, you could really start making some powerful mobile sites for media outlets and venues. The only thing this chapter could have really used is a picture gallery for artists and venues. But, don't worry; we'll approach that in the next chapter where we'll be creating a showcase for photographers.

7
Fully Responsive Photography

Our mobile phones are quickly becoming our photo albums. Photographers represent a somewhat untapped market for mobile web development. But if you think about it, this market should have been the first to adapt to the mobile world. With the saturation of smartphones in developed nations, e-mail open rates on smartphones are rapidly approaching 40 percent and may be there by the time you read this (`http://www.emailmonday.com/mobile-email-usage-statistics`).

When you get that e-mail from your photographer that your photos are ready for viewing, aren't you so excited that you try to view them immediately? Yet there are a LOT of photographers who are masters at their trade that do not have websites that are ready to meet the new mobile demands:

So, here's what we'll cover in this chapter:

- Creating a basic gallery using PhotoSwipe
- Supporting the full range of device sizes – responsive web design
- Text readability in responsive design
- Sending back only what is needed – RESS

Creating a basic gallery using PhotoSwipe

If you're looking for the single fastest way to create a photo gallery, you're not going to come up with any faster solution than PhotoSwipe (`http://www.photoswipe.com/`). Weighing in at 82 K, it's not exactly light but it works on pretty much anything that jQuery Mobile supports as either A or B grade. Their site says it works with any WebKit-based browser. That pretty much means iOS, Android, and BlackBerry. The big three are covered. But what about Windows Phone? Good news! It seems to work great there too. Even with JavaScript turned off, PhotoSwipe degrades gracefully to a reasonable page-by-page experience. We could start from scratch and make a pure jQuery Mobile experience but, really… why?

Once again I'm going to dispense with the academically correct behavior of perfectly separating JavaScript and CSS into their own files, and simply build all customized JavaScript into the page itself. It's just easier for the purposes of this book. I'm assuming if you're reading this, that you already know how to separate things properly and why.

Let's start with the basics. For the most part, this is boilerplate from their site but we're starting with our own images from the photographer:

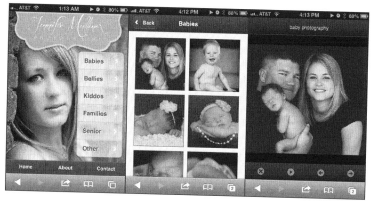

Let's start with the key portions of the `<head>` tag:

```html
<link rel="stylesheet" href="http://code.jquery.com/mobile/1.3.0/
jquery.mobile-1.3.0.min.css" />
<link rel="stylesheet" href="mullinax.min.css" />
<link rel="stylesheet" href="photoswipe.css" />
<link rel="stylesheet" href="jquery-mobile.css" />

<script src="js/klass.min.js"></script>
<script src="http://code.jquery.com/jquery-1.8.2.min.js"></script>
<script src="http://code.jquery.com/mobile/1.3.0/jquery.mobile-
1.3.0.min.js"></script>
<script src="js/code.photoswipe.jquery-3.0.5.min.js"></script>
<script src="js/code.photoswipe.galleryinit.js"></script>
```

Take note that we are now using a custom theme built with **ThemeRoller** (`http://jquerymobile.com/themeroller/`). Therefore, we are only using `jquery.mobile.structure-1.2.0.min.css` instead of the full jQM CSS. The `mullinax.min.css` file was produced by ThemeRoller and contains everything else needed apart from the structure CSS.

The files `photoswipe.css`, `jquery-mobile.css`, `klass.min.js`, and `code.photoswipe.jquery-3.0.5.min.js` are all part of the of the PhotoSwipe boilerplate. The filename, `jquery-mobile.css`, is a little misleading. It's actually more like an adapter stylesheet to make PhotoSwipe work and look right in jQuery Mobile. Without it, your gallery's unordered lists won't look right. Initially, there's not a lot in there:

```css
.gallery {
list-style: none;
padding: 0;
margin: 0;
}
.gallery:after {
clear: both;
content: ".";
display: block;
height: 0;
visibility: hidden;
}
.gallery li {
float: left;
width: 33.33333333%;
}
```

```
.gallery li a {
display: block;
margin: 5px;
border: 1px solid #3c3c3c;
}
.gallery li img {
display: block;
width: 100%;
height: auto;
}
#Gallery1 .ui-content, #Gallery2 .ui-content {
overflow: hidden;
}
```

This setup is OK on an iPhone or Android phones but if you're looking at it on any kind of a tablet- or desktop-size browser, the thumbnails of the gallery could get annoyingly large. Let's see what we can do with a touch of media queries to give it a more responsive design.

Supporting the full range of device sizes – responsive web design

Responsive web design (RWD) is the concept of making a single page work for every device size. That means, we're not just talking about mobile phones with a 3.5-inch screen. That's only the beginning. We are going to support tablets of all sizes, and even desktop resolutions. For more on the concept of RWD, check out `http://en.wikipedia.org/wiki/Responsive_web_design`.

In order to make RWD work, let's set a few breakpoints based on common devices and resolution breakpoints. I'm going to start by redefining the default gallery item size to 50 percent. Why? It just feels more comfortable to me while browsing on a smartphone in portrait mode. So, here are the breakpoints. Let's put them into `chapter7.css`:

```
.gallery li {
float: left; width: 50%; }

/* iPhone Horizontal --------------------*/
@media all and (min-width: 480px){
.gallery li { width: 33.33333333%; }
}
```

```
/* iPad Vertical ---------------------*/
@media only screen and (min-width: 768px) {
.gallery li { width: 20%; }
}

/* iPad Horizontal --------------------*/
@media only screen and (min-width: 1024px) {
.gallery li { width: 16.66666666%; }
}

/* Nexus 7 Horizontal ----------------*/
@media only screen and (min-width: 1280px) {
.gallery li { width: 14.285714%; }
}

/* Laptop 1440 -----------------------*/
@media only screen and (min-width: 1440px) {
.gallery li { width: 12.5%; }
}

/* Monitor 1600 ----------------------*/
@media only screen and (min-width: 1600px) {
.gallery li { width: 11.111111%; }
}

/* Monitor 1920 ----------------------*/
@media only screen and (min-width: 1920px) {
.gallery li { width: 10%; }
}
```

As I was testing this setup, I carefully considered the average viewing distance between myself and whatever screen I was viewing. These breakdowns resulted in roughly the same percentage of the field of view for a thumbnail that seemed ideal. Obviously, my focus group of one means nothing from a scientific perspective so tweak to your heart's content.

It could be asked, why not just make each image a fixed size? Why the different resolution breakpoints? Pretty simple really, it keeps thing evenly spaced instead of having a major gap on one side because some monitors' or browsers' resizing had just enough room to force a line break but not take up the slack. It also has the added benefit, for the book, of showing you a good way to break down a universal stylesheet to turn a jQuery Mobile site into a universal site using media queries. Any other resolution-based tweaks we want to make can be put right into chapter7.css in its appropriate place.

The script `code.photoswipe.galleryinit.js` is present on the PhotoSwipe gallery page itself within the downloadable example. I don't think it will ever need to be edited or customized on a per page basis so I've extracted that chuck of script into `code.photoswipe.galleryinit.js`. Here is the code. Think nothing more of it since it is now off in its own little file never to be seen or heard from again:

```
(function(window, $, PhotoSwipe){
$(document).ready(function(){
  $(document)
    .on('pageshow', 'div.gallery-page', function(e){
      var  currentPage = $(e.target),
      options = {},
      photoSwipeInstance = $("ul.gallery a", e.target)
      .photoSwipe(options,  currentPage.attr('id'));
      return true;
    })
    .on('pagehide', 'div.gallery-page', function(e){
      var currentPage = $(e.target),
      photoSwipeInstance =
      PhotoSwipe.getInstance(currentPage.attr('id'));
      if (typeof photoSwipeInstance != "undefined"
      && photoSwipeInstance != null) {
        PhotoSwipe.detatch(photoSwipeInstance);
      }
      return true;
    });
});
} (window, window.jQuery, window.Code.PhotoSwipe));
```

Now, let us now consider some of the "pages" themselves. We'll be putting this code, and evolving it as we go, in the `index.html` file:

```
<div id="gallery" data-role="page">
  <div class="logoContainer">
    <img class="logo" src="images/logo.png" alt="Mullinax Photography"
/>
  </div>
  <div data-role="content">
    <div class="artisticNav">
      <ul data-role="listview" data-inset="true">
        <li><a href="#babies">Babies</a></li>
        <li><a href="#babies">Bellies</a></li>
        <li><a href="#babies">Kiddos</a></li>
        <li><a href="#babies">Families</a></li>
        <li><a href="#babies">Senior</a></li>
        <li><a href="#babies">Other</a></li>
```

```
            </ul>
          </div>
        </div><!-- /content -->
    </div><!-- /page -->
```

The design concepts for the gallery screen are as follows:

- Full screen photo background
- Centered logo on small screens taking up no more than 90 percent of the width of the screen and not growing beyond its original size
- The navigation should still be obvious but not get in the way of the art itself

Here's the relevant CSS that we are also putting into `chapter7.css`:

```
.logoContainer{text-align:center;}
.logoContainer img{width:90%; max-width:438px;}

#gallery{
background-image:url(backgroundSmall.jpg);
background-repeat:no-repeat;
background-position: top center;
}

.portrait #gallery{
background-size:auto 100% !important;
}

.landscape #gallery{
background-size:100% auto !important;
}

#gallery .ui-btn-up-c {
background: rgba(255,255,255,.1);
text-shadow: 1px 1px 0 white;
background-image: -webkit-gradient(linear,left top,left bottom,from(
rgba(255,255,255,.5) ),to( rgba(255,255,255,.7) ));
background-image: -webkit-linear-gradient( rgba(255,255,255,.5),rg
ba(255,255,255,.7) );
background-image: -moz-linear-gradient( rgba(255,255,255,.5),rg
ba(255,255,255,.7) );
background-image: -ms-linear-gradient( rgba(255,255,255,.5),rg
ba(255,255,255,.7) );
background-image: -o-linear-gradient( rgba(255,255,255,.5),rg
ba(255,255,255,.7) );
background-image: linear-gradient( rgba(255,255,255,.5),rg
ba(255,255,255,.7) );
}

#galleryNav{ position:absolute; bottom:10px; right:10px; }
```

Now we just need a little JavaScript to tie this all together. When the orientation changes, we want to change which direction gets the 100 percent of the width for the background:

```
/*Whenever the orientation changes*/
$(window).on("orientationchange", function(event){
  $("body").removeClass("portrait")
    .removeClass("landscape")
    .addClass(event.orientation);
});


/*Prime the body with the orientation on document.ready*/
$(document).ready(function(e) {
  if($(window).width() > $(window).height())
    $("body").addClass("landscape")
  else
    $("body").addClass("portrait")
});
```

That's good enough for our gallery entry page, now let's put together a sample gallery for baby photos. There are many entries for the gallery in the code of this chapter. However, for brevity's sake I've shortened the code here. Again, this will be in the final version of `index.html` in the code files:

```
<div data-role="page" data-add-back-btn="true" id="babies"
class="gallery-page">
  <div data-role="header">
    <h1>Babies</h1>
  </div>
  <div data-role="content">
    <ul class="gallery">
      <li><a href="images/full/babies1.jpg" rel="external"><img
src="images/thumb/babies1.jpg" alt="001" /></a></li>
      <li><a href="images/full/babies2.jpg" rel="external"><img
src="images/thumb/babies2.jpg" alt="002" /></a></li>
      <li><a href="images/full/babies3.jpg" rel="external"><img
src="images/thumb/babies3.jpg" alt="003" /></a></li>
      <li><a href="images/full/babies26.jpg" rel="external"><img
src="images/thumb/babies26.jpg" alt="026" /></a></li>
    </ul>
  </div>
</div>
```

If you do not put a `rel="external"` on each of the links to the images, it will not work properly. The PhotoSwipe documentation made that pretty clear. If you're not yet familiar with `rel="external"`, it is a way to tell jQuery Mobile to *not* follow the link with its usual AJAX-based navigation. As such, it will force a full-page load to whatever you're linking to.

Now, just for the fun of it, open this in a desktop browser at full width and then shrink it down to mobile size and watch it adapt. Try out the gallery landing page, the baby thumbnail gallery, and the slideshow that PhotoSwipe provides.

One of the cool parts about PhotoSwipe is that even if you've disabled zooming on your mobile site using the meta-viewport tag, the user is still able to pinch and zoom around the full-sized photos. This is really nice on a tablet. All they have to do to get back to the navigation is to double tap the image and it will zoom to its original size and reveal the navigation. Not the most obvious thing but the back button works as well.

Naturally, as the name may suggest, you can simply swipe from photo to photo and it will loop back around to the beginning of the set once it reaches the end. There is also a slideshow feature that will run indefinitely. In both of these cases, if the user presses the back button, they'll be taken back to the thumbnails page.

The only real problem that we have at this point is that we have a site that scales well but the background images and full-sized photos might be larger than strictly necessary. The background image isn't really a problem because we can govern which size to send back based on our media queries. We just need to create two or three background images sizes and override which image is used in the `jquery-bile.css` file. In the final version of the code for this chapter I have renamed `jquery-mobile.css` to `chapter7.css` to avoid any confusion with actual jQuery Mobile library CSS files.

Text readability and responsive design

Studies have shown that there are ideal character limits per line. Ideally, you should settle on 35, 55, 75, or 95 CPL (characters per line). People tend to prefer either shorter or longer lines. Since we're really trying to showcase photography here, let's go with the shorter CPL. If you want to read the full report, you can find it at `http://psychology.wichita.edu/surl/usabilitynews/72/LineLength.asp`.

To a large extent, the width of our text columns will be dictated by the devices themselves. On smaller devices, we really have no choice but to go a 100% width. Once we get to tablets in landscape mode, we'll have room to do creative things with our text. We could, for larger widths, increase our CPL to 55 and it would look great. We may also consider using larger images as well. Whatever we do, having a strong set of media query breakpoints is the key.

Let's take some paragraphs of text about sessions and make it more responsive with this study as a guideline:

```
<div id="sessions" data-role="page">
  <div class="logoContainer">
    <a href="#home"><img class="logo" src="images/logo.png"
alt="Mullinax Photography" border="0" /></a>
  </div>
<div data-role="content">
  <div class="textContainer ui-shadow">
    <h3>For Your Session</h3>

    <p>Portrait sessions may be held at our Western Shawnee Studio,
in the comfort of your home, or a location of your choice. I love
capturing little ones in their natural environment. At home, children
often feel more comfortable and are more likely to play and have fun.
It's the perfect environment for capturing those sweet little smiles
and laughs that you as a parent adore!!</p>

    <p>I strive to make each portrait session relaxed, fun, and
beautiful. Like each child, each session will be unique to fit your
family's needs. As a mother, I understand firsthand the challenges
that come with photographing little ones. The perfect portrait can
take time. Being the perfect model is hard work and often breaks
are needed.  That is why each of my sessions is held without time
constraints. A one-of-a-kind portrait cannot be rushed!! While I don't
want to overstay my welcome, I do want to stay long enough that you
and I are both satisfied with the portraits that were captured.</p>

    <h3>After Your Session</h3>

    <p>Approximately two weeks after your session, I will post an
online gallery for you to view your proofs as well as share with
friends and family. Your proof gallery will stay online for 10 days.
At this time you have the option of placing your order through the
website using our shopping cart or you can schedule an in-person
appointment.</p>
```

```
      </div>
    </div><!-- /content -->
    <div data-role="footer">
      <div data-role="navbar" data-position="fixed">
        <ul>
          <li><a href="#home">Home</a></li>
          <li><a href="#about">About</a></li>
          <li><a href="#contact">Contact</a></li>
        </ul>
      </div><!-- /navbar -->
    </div>
  </div><!-- /page -->
```

Next, let's create some of the rules around its placement on the page:

```
#sessions{
  background-color:#888;
  background-repeat:no-repeat;
  background-position:
  center center;
}

#sessions h3{
  font-family: 'Euphoria Script', Helvetica, sans-serif;
  font-size:200%;
  font-weight:bold;
  margin:0;
}

.textContainer{
  background-color:#EEE;
  margin:-5px;
}

/* iPhone Portrait --*/
@media all and (min-width: 320px){
  .textContainer{
    padding:120px 10px 10px 10px;
  }
  #sessions{
    background-image:none;
  }
}
```

```
/* iPad Verticle --*/
@media only screen and (min-width: 768px) {
.textContainer{ padding:160px 10px 10px 10px;}
}


/* iPad Horizontal --*/
@media only screen and (min-width: 1024px) {
  .textContainer{
    float:right;
    width:35em;
    padding:2em 2em 2em 2em;
    height:550px;
    overflow:scroll;
  }
  #sessions{
    background-image:url(images/Colleen.jpeg)
  }
}


/* Laptop 1440 --*/
@media only screen and (min-width: 1440px) {
  #sessions{
    background-image:url(images/Gliser.jpg)
  }
}
```

As before, a rule set in the lower widths will carry through to the wider widths unless a value is specified to override. You can see how I'm switching out the images used on sessions for iPad landscape view and 1440 resolutions. Before those, every resolution inherited the `background-image:none` form and the 320px rules.

Now let's take a look at our results.

Smartphone-sized devices

Here we see the session content on small screens for both portrait and horizontal orientation. Either way is highly readable but neither is really ideal for displaying anything other than the text. If we tried to squeeze in any kind of artwork, it just wouldn't show up well. We'd be violating the good text readability we just talked about. Either you or the photographer might think that perhaps having one of their images faded in the background would look good but DON'T! Leave the majority of the reading text as black on white in standard size fonts with standard fonts:

Tablet-sized devices

Here we see the same thing rendered on tablets. On portrait orientation, it's still great for reading if we leave the text at a `100%` width. We are well within the guidelines for good readability. However, that breaks down when the user switches to landscape. In landscape, tablets finally have enough room to show some photography and the text as well:

Desktop-sized devices

This is still a jQuery Mobile page but we're looking more like a desktop site. Now we can show more than just one face so we might as well switch out some different photos to showcase the artist's ability:

Yes, this is me and my family. Yes, I *am* very proud of them. And I'm pretty happy with the way the text treatment is working out on each of these resolution breakpoints and that it's all one page.

Cycling background images

So, how do we cycle background images when the very images we're using depend on our current resolution and orientation? That pretty much rules out cycling out a single image. Instead we're going to have to swap out entire stylesheets. Here we go:

```
<link rel="stylesheet" href="rotating0.css" id="rotatingBackgrounds" />
```

It's a pretty simple stylesheet to begin with but you could make it as complex as you like. We're not accounting for HD display versus SD displays for now. The iPhone 4 with Retina display (326 ppi) was released in June of 2010. Ever since, the trend is moving toward HD screens anyway, so I'm simply assuming most people have updated their smartphone within the last two years and that they either have a high resolution screen or very soon will. Keep in mind also that we are on the edge of the LTE (fourth generation mobile broadband) ubiquity. That means that very soon, mobile will be faster than most home broadband speeds.

Now, is this really an excuse for laziness and not making smaller versions to capitalize on performance where you can? No, and most likely, some haters and academics will even take issue with the previous paragraph. I will say this, performance does matter. It is a billable feature. But think about how many images you want to be cycling through and then multiply that by how many resolution and dimension variants you want to spend time preparing and testing. Again, it's all billable unless you're doing it for free.

How much longer until such minute optimizations really makes no discernible difference? If you're reading this in 2014 or later, you might already be scoffing at the idea of having to worry about bandwidth in any practical sense (depending on your market). Just some food for thought.

Here's one of the CSS files for the rotation:

```
@charset "UTF-8";
/* CSS Document */

#gallery{background-image:url(images/homebg.jpg);}

/* iPhone Portrait --*/
@media all and (min-width: 320px){
#home{
background-image:url(images/backgroundSmartphone.jpg);
}
#sessions{ background-image:none; }
}

/* iPhone Horizontal / Some Droids --*/
@media all and (min-width: 480px){   }

/* iPad Verticle --*/
@media only screen and (min-width: 768px) {
#home{background-image:url(images/backgroundSmall.jpg);}
}
```

```
/* iPad Horizontal --*/
@media only screen and (min-width: 1024px) {
#sessions{ background-image:url(images/Colleen.jpeg) }
}

/* Nexus 7 Horizontal --*/
@media only screen and (min-width: 1280px) {  }

/* Laptop 1440 --*/
@media only screen and (min-width: 1440px) {
#sessions{ background-image:url(images/Gliser.jpg) }
}

/* Monitor 1600 --*/
@media only screen and (min-width: 1600px) {  }

/* Monitor 1920 --*/
@media only screen and (min-width: 1920px) {  }
```

Now that we've got that, we need to decide how we'll cycle them. We could use a setInterval JavaScript to swap the stylesheets out on a timer. Honestly, even for a photography website, I think that's being a bit optimistic. We probably wouldn't want to swap any faster than once every 5 seconds. Think about it: the mobile usage pattern involves quick, short bursts of productivity or gaming. Most people are not going to stay on any given mobile screen for more than 5 seconds unless it is either text-heavy, like an article, or is so poorly crafted that the user is having trouble navigating. So, it's pretty safe to say that the setInterval option is right out.

OK, so, maybe it's best to randomly choose a stylesheet on the pagebeforeshow event? Consider the following code:

```
$(document).on("pagebeforeshow", "[data-role='page']", function(){
    $("#rotatingBackgrounds").attr("href", "rotating" +
Math.floor(Math.random()*4) + ".css");
});
```

But what happens when we try this? We get strange, ugly image blinks. With fade transitions or slides, it really doesn't matter. Using the pageshow event makes no difference either. It looks terrible. Do not do it. I know it's tempting but it won't look good at all. *So, after all this, it's my recommendation to keep a single, randomly assigned, per-session stylesheet.* Consider the following code snippet:

```
<link rel="stylesheet" href="" id="rotatingBackgrounds" />
<script type="text/javascript">
$("#rotatingBackgrounds")
```

```
    .attr("href","rotating"+Math.floor(Math.random()*4)+".css")
</script>
```

Notice that I did not simply use `document.write()`.

Pro Tip

Never ever ever... ever use `document.write()` in a jQuery Mobile environment. It can play HELL with your DOM and you'll be scratching your head wondering what went wrong. I've seen it bite people before. My friend's already thin hair was in full retreat from the head scratching this problem was causing him. Trust me, `document.write()` is to be avoided.

Another responsive approach – RESS

Responsive Design + Server Side Components (RESS) is an idea that makes a lot of sense. The concept is that you use a server-side mobile detection method such as **WURFL** (`http://wurfl.sourceforge.net/`). Then you send up a different version of page components, different sized images, and so on. We could then change the wrappers around the page content and the navigation to use jQuery Mobile just as easily as any home-brewed markup. The beauty of this approach is that everybody gets the content that is right for them without the bloat of typical responsive design and it's always on the same URL.

The first time I saw this idea proposed in writing was in an article at `http://www.lukew.com/ff/entry.asp?1392` by Luke Wroblewski (`https://twitter.com/lukew`) in September 2011. In it, he outlines the very performance problem we now face with images. Luke meant this as a way of doing pure responsive web design without any kind of mobile framework.

WURFL can tell you the screen size of the device you're serving and you could resize (on the fly) your photographer's original 3 MB image, down to maybe 150 K, 70 K, and so on, depending on the device resolution. You'd still want to be sure to make it about twice as large as the screen size you're serving or the user will only see a blurry mess when then try to zoom in on their photo in the PhotoSwipe view.

While handy in some ways, RESS will never be a perfect solution because it depends on browser sniffing to do its work. Is that so bad? No, not really. No solution is perfect, but the database of devices is community driven and rapidly updated so that helps. This would be a very viable solution and we'll discuss it more in depth in the next chapter.

The final code

The full code for this experience is a little on the verbose side for putting into a book and we've already explored the concepts around it. I would strongly encourage you to look at the code. At this point, there should be nothing surprising to you. Play with it. Adapt it. Go get yourself some free photography by trading services to build your portfolio.

Summary

Tackling responsive design with a mobile-first approach, as we have here, can take what is a great mobile site and make a highly performant desktop site but it doesn't usually work the other way around. The key to it all is the media queries and starting small first. If it works that well on mobile with the limited processor, bandwidth, and network latency, think how amazing it will be on a machine where none of the restraints exist. In the next chapter we'll examine WURFL and other mobile detection methods to try and adapt existing websites and make them mobile.

8
Integrating jQuery Mobile into Existing Sites

We can't all be so lucky enough to only work on new sites. Maybe the customer is unwilling to pay for a mobile-first site or maybe they like their desktop site as it is and just want a mobile site. Your mobile implementation could be the gateway to future business with the client. We need to be ready with a few techniques to wedge jQuery Mobile into their existing site.

What we'll cover is as follows:

- Detecting mobile – server-side, client-side, and the combination of the two
- Mobilizing full site pages – the hard way
- Mobilizing full site pages – the easy way

Detecting mobile – server-side, client-side, and the combination of the two

Not everyone is doing responsive design so there's a pretty good chance you're going to need to know how to detect mobile devices. We've approached the topic lightly before but now let's get serious.

Browser sniffing versus feature detection

This topic has the potential to start a geek war. On one side you have people who proclaim the virtues of community-maintained databases that perform mobile detection on the server side. WURFL is a prime example. Using it, we can get a lot of information about the device that is visiting our sites. Listing it all here would just be a waste of space. Check out `http://www.tera-wurfl.com/explore/index.php` to see it in action or view the entire list of capabilities at `http://www.scientiamobile.com/wurflCapability/`.

On the other side of the debate, people point out that the server-side detection (even when it is database driven) can lead to brand new devices not being recognized until they're in the database and the site administrator updates their local copy. This is not completely true. All Androids say so. It is the same with iPhone, iPad, Blackberry, and Microsoft. Still, a much more future-friendly (`http://futurefriend.ly/`) approach is to use feature detection. For instance, does the device support canvas or perhaps touch events? Almost certainly, if you support such technologies and events, you're primed for a mobile experience with jQuery Mobile.

Regardless, at this point we're going to assume that we're working with a company that already has a website and now wants a mobile site too. Therefore, we'll need to be able to detect mobile and route them to the correct site.

WURFL – server-side database-driven browser sniffing

WURFL has APIs for Java, PHP, and .NET. Pick up a copy of the version that works for you at `http://wurfl.sourceforge.net/apis.php`. Since virtually every single hosting provider out there supports PHP out of the box, we're going to go with the PHP example:

I simply used the built-in server that comes on Mac OS X but you could also use MAMP (`http://www.mamp.info/en/index.html`). You can easily run the example on any hosting platform such as 1&1, GoDaddy, Host Gator, take your pick. If you want to try the examples on your own Windows computer, you can use XAMPP (`http://www.apachefriends.org/en/xampp.html`) or WAMP (`http://www.wampserver.com/en/`) as a quick shortcut. I'm not going to get into the particulars of server setup and environment configuration in this book. That could probably justify a book of its own.

So, PHP... here we go. Start at `http://wurfl.sourceforge.net/php_index.php`. From there you can download the latest copy of **WURFL API package** and unzip it. Take the entire unzipped folder and dump it anywhere in your site. If all is well, you should be able to hit the demo page and see details about your browser and device. On my Mac, it was `http://127.0.0.1/~sgliser/wurfl-php/examples/demo/index.php` but your path will vary.

When you run the default example, you can instantly see how useful it is, but let's make it even better. This version I created puts the most useful at the top and lists all other options below:

```php
<?php
    // Move the configuration and initialization to
    // the tip so you can use it in the head.

    // Include the configuration file
    include_once './inc/wurfl_config_standard.php';

    $wurflInfo = $wurflManager->getWURFLInfo();

    if (isset($_GET['ua']) && trim($_GET['ua'])) {
        $ua = $_GET['ua'];
        $requestingDevice = $wurflManager->getDeviceForUserAgent($_
GET['ua']);
    } else {
        $ua = $_SERVER['HTTP_USER_AGENT'];

        //This line detects the visiting device by looking
        //at its HTTP Request ($_SERVER)

        $requestingDevice = $wurflManager->getDeviceForHttpRequest($_
SERVER); } ?>

<html>
    <head>
        <title>WURFL PHP API Example</title>
```

```php
        <?php if($requestingDevice->getCapability('mobile_browser') !==
"") { ?>
        <meta name="viewport" content="width=device-width, initial-
scale=1, maximum-scale=1.0, user-scalable=no">
        <link rel="stylesheet" href="http://code.jquery.com/
mobile/1.2.0/jquery.mobile-1.2.0.min.css" />
        <script src="http://code.jquery.com/jquery-1.8.2.min.js"></
script>
        <script src="http://code.jquery.com/mobile/1.2.0/jquery.mobile-
1.2.0.min.js"></script>
    <?php } ?>
  </head>
  <body>
```

Here we create the only real page, in a jQuery Mobile fashion:

```php
    <div data-role="page">
      <div data-role="header">
        <h1>WURFL XML INFO</h1>
      </div>
      <div data-role="content" id="content">

      <h4>VERSION: <?php echo $wurflInfo->version; ?> </h4>
      <p>User Agent: <b> <?php echo htmlspecialchars($ua); ?> </b></p>
      <ul data-role="listview">
        <li data-role="list-divider">
          <h2>Very Useful</h2>
        </li>
        <li>Brand Name: <?php echo $requestingDevice-
>getCapability('brand_name'); ?> </li>
        <li>Model Name: <?php echo $requestingDevice-
>getCapability('model_name'); ?> </li>
        <li>Is Wireless Device: <?php echo $requestingDevice-
>getCapability('is_wireless_device'); ?></li>
        <li>Mobile:
        <?php if($requestingDevice->getCapability('mobile_browser') !==
"") {
          echo "true";
        }else{
          echo "false";
        }; ?>
        </li>
        <li>Tablet: <?php echo $requestingDevice->getCapability('is_
tablet'); ?> </li>
        <li>Pointing Method: <?php echo $requestingDevice-
>getCapability('pointing_method'); ?> </li>
```

```
    <li>Resolution Width: <?php echo $requestingDevice-
>getCapability('resolution_width'); ?> </li>
    <li>Resolution Height: <?php echo $requestingDevice-
>getCapability('resolution_height'); ?> </li>
    <li>Marketing Name: <?php echo $requestingDevice-
>getCapability('marketing_name'); ?> </li>
    <li>Preferred Markup: <?php echo $requestingDevice-
>getCapability('preferred_markup'); ?> </li>
```

Here we start listing out the entire set of known data from WURFL simply by looping through the array of properties:

```
    <li data-role="list-divider">
      <h2>All Capabilities</h2>
    </li>

    <?php foreach(array_keys($requestingDevice->getAllCapabilities())
as $capabilityName){ ?>
      <li><?php echo "<h3>" .$capabilityName."</h3><p>"
.$requestingDevice->getCapability($capabilityName)."</p>"; ?>
      </li>
    <?php } ?>
    </ul>

    <p><b>Query WURFL by providing the user agent:</b></p>
    <form method="get" action="index.php">
      <div>User Agent: <input type="text" name="ua" size="100"
value="<?php echo isset($_GET['ua'])? htmlspecialchars($_GET['ua']):
''; ?>" />
        <input type="submit" value="submit" />
      </div>
    </form>
  </div>
</div>
</body>
</html>
```

 Note, we've *conditionally* made this a jQuery Mobile page by using the server-side detection to see if the user is mobile. Only then do we inject the jQM libraries.

The attributes under the *Very Useful* section are probably all you really need for most day-to-day work but be sure you at least skim over the other options. The most useful features are as follows:

- `is_wireless_device`
- `mobile_browser`
- `is_tablet`
- `pointing_method`
- `resolution_width`
- `resolution_height`

Now, granted, this does not tell us everything about the browser/device. For instance, an iPhone 4S or 5 will be recognized as an original iPhone. There's also no distinguishing the iPad mini using WURFL. This is because the user agents have never been updated as the Apple devices have evolved. WURFL has no way of knowing that a device has a high pixel density and should thus be sent higher resolution images. Therefore, we'll still need to use media queries to determine pixel ratios and adapt our graphics appropriately. Here is a brief example:

```
.logo-large{
  background-image:url(../images/logo.png);
  background-repeat:no-repeat;
  background-position:0 0;
  position:relative;
  top:0;
  left:0;
  width:290px;
  height:65px;
  margin:0 auto;
  border:none;
}


/* HD / Retina ----------------------------------------------*/ @media
only screen and (-webkit-min-device-pixel-ratio: 1.5),
      only screen and (min--moz-device-pixel-ratio: 1.5),
      only screen and (min-resolution: 240dpi)
{
  .logo-large{
    background-image:url(../images/logoHD.png);
    background-size:290px 65px;
  }
}
```

Using media queries is pretty much the only way to detect an iPad mini. It has the same resolution as the iPad 2, just in a smaller format. However, as we can see from the preceding code, we can qualify a media query using DPI. The iPad 2 has 132 dpi. The iPad mini has 163. For more on this, check out http://www.mobilexweb.com/blog/ipad-mini-detection-for-html5-user-agent.

So far, we've pretty much assumed smartphones but remember that jQuery Mobile is a framework that is also perfect for ... not-so-smart-phones. You may have customers in a market that is not as developed and uses cell connections for nearly everything. There may not be as many JavaScript-enabled touchscreen phones there. In a case like that, you won't be able to use JavaScript-based feature detection. Very quickly, WURFL or some other server-side detection will become your only reasonable option for detecting wireless devices and serving them up something useful.

JavaScript-based browser sniffing

It is arguable that this may be (academically) the worst possible way to detect mobile but it does have its virtues. This pragmatic example is very useful in that it gives you a lot of options. Perhaps our budget is limited and so we've only tested for certain devices. We want to be sure we're only letting in people that we know will have a good experience. Case in point: no BlackBerry device below Version 6 will be allowed because we've chosen to do some fancy JavaScript templating that Version 5 and lower just can't handle. Perhaps we've also not taken the time yet to optimize for tablets but in the mean time we can start providing a better experience for any smartphones. In any case, this could come in quite useful:

```
<script type="text/javascript">
  var agent = navigator.userAgent;
  var isWebkit = (agent.indexOf("AppleWebKit") > 0);
  var isIPad = (agent.indexOf("iPad") > 0);
  var isIOS = (agent.indexOf("iPhone") > 0 || agent.indexOf("iPod") >
0);
  var isAndroid = (agent.indexOf("Android")  > 0);
  var isNewBlackBerry = (agent.indexOf("AppleWebKit") > 0 && agent.
indexOf("BlackBerry") > 0);
  var isWebOS = (agent.indexOf("webOS") > 0);
  var isWindowsMobile = (agent.indexOf("IEMobile") > 0);
  var isSmallScreen = (screen.width < 767 || (isAndroid && screen.
width < 1000));
  var isUnknownMobile = (isWebkit && isSmallScreen);
  var isMobile = (isIOS || isAndroid || isNewBlackBerry || isWebOS ||
isWindowsMobile || isUnknownMobile);
  var isTablet = (isIPad || (isMobile && !isSmallScreen));
```

```
if ( isMobile && isSmallScreen && document.cookie.indexOf(
"mobileFullSiteClicked=") < 0 ) mobileRedirect();
</script>
```

We've done a little work here to future-proof the detection by creating a classification for unknown mobile devices as being anything running WebKit that has a small screen. Chances are, any new platforms that come out will be using WebKit as its browser. Microsoft is the only exception that still seems to think it has something more to offer on its own and their platform is easy enough to sniff. This approach, while flexible, would require direct intervention if a new platform was launched without a WebKit browser. But, that doesn't happen very often. Even if it does, it would take a while for that platform to gain a critical mass worth considering. If you're going by the 80/20 rule (worry about reaching 80 percent successfully and reach the last 20 percent when you can), this gets you well into the upper 90s.

JavaScript-based feature detection using Modernizr

There are several ways that you can perform feature detection. Probably the easiest way is to use a tool such as Modernizr (`http://modernizr.com/`). You can customize a download to only detect the features that you care about. If you want to do HTML5 audio/video, it might be nice to know if you can:

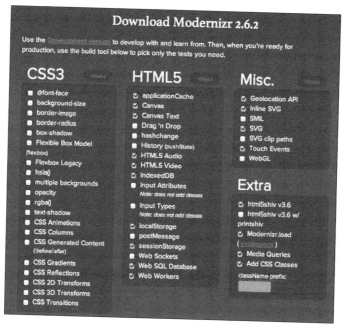

The platform is not exactly light. Just the options shown in the preceding screenshot led to a 12 K minified JS. But hey, we throw around images of that size like they're nothing. At least a JavaScript library is useful. This still won't tell you if the user coming to you is mobile but is that even the right question to be asking?

Perhaps, all we need to know is that the device we're looking at supports touch events. The other options are great for knowing what you can and cannot do but if the user interface is touch, even if it's a tablet or a full-sized touch based monitor, give the user the interface they deserve. Give them jQuery Mobile.

JavaScript-based lean feature detection

This useful little snippet of code is something cobbled together for detecting mobile. It is a blending of feature detection and browser sniffing. Most modern smartphones will support all the event and APIs we're looking for here. Microsoft, being the special case they always seem to be, has to be browser sniffed. According to their Windows Phone developer blog, you can simply check the user agent for IEMobile. Fair enough, here's the result:

```
if(
    ('querySelector' in document
    && 'localStorage' in window
    && 'addEventListener' in window
    && ('ontouchstart' in window ||
    window.DocumentTouch && document instanceof DocumentTouch)
    )

    || navigator.userAgent.indexOf('IEMobile') > 0)
{
    location.replace('YOUR MOBILE SITE');
}
```

If for some reason we decided that we didn't want to send tablets to our jQM masterpieces, we could always throw in some of the other tests from the previous section.

Server-side plus client-side detection

Here's an idea, when the user first hits your server, send them a page whose only job is to run Modernizer and then send the resulting capabilities back to the server so all collected knowledge is in one place.

This file is `test.html` in the code files package for the chapter:

```html
<!doctype html>
<html>
<head>
  <style type="text/css">

    #sd{display:block;} /*standard def*/
    #hd{display:none;} /*high dev*/

    @media only screen and
      (-webkit-min-device-pixel-ratio: 1.5),
      only screen and (min--moz-device-pixel-ratio: 1.5),
      only screen and (min-resolution: 240dpi) {
        #sd{display:none;} /*standard def*/
        #hd{display:block;} /*high dev*/
      }
  </style>
  <script type="text/javascript" src="modernizr.custom.94279.js"></script>
  <script type="text/javascript" src="https://ajax.googleapis.com/ajax/libs/jquery/1.8.3/jquery.min.js"></script>
  <meta charset="UTF-8">
  <title>Loading</title>
</head>
<body>
  <div id="hd"></div>
  <div id="sd"></div>
</body>
<script type="text/javascript">
  if($("#hd").is(":visible")){
    $("html").addClass("hdpi");
  }else{
    $("html").addClass("sdpi");
  }

  $.post("/~sgliser/wurfl-php/examples/demo/session_set.php",
    {
      modernizrData: $("html").attr("class")
    }
  )
  .success(function(data, textStatus, jqXHR) {
    console.log(data);
```

```
    location.replace("YOUR MOBILE SITE");   })
   .error(function(jqXHR, textStatus, errorThrown) {
     console.log(errorThrown);
     location.replace("SOMEWHERE ELSE");
   });
 </script>
 </html>
```

Just to make the circle complete. Here is a version of the WURFL detection scripts that will return the values as JSON so we can store it to HTML5 `sessionStorage`. This file is found at `/wurfl-php/examples/demo/session_set.php`:

```php
<?php session_start();

// Move the configuration and initialization
// to the tip so you can use it in the head.

// Include the configuration file

include_once './inc/wurfl_config_standard.php';

$wurflInfo = $wurflManager->getWURFLInfo();

if (isset($_GET['ua']) && trim($_GET['ua'])) {
   $ua = $_GET['ua'];
   $requestingDevice = $wurflManager->getDeviceForUserAgent($_
GET['ua']);
} else {
   $ua = $_SERVER['HTTP_USER_AGENT'];

   // This line detects the visiting device by looking
   // at its HTTP Request ($_SERVER)

   $requestingDevice = $wurflManager->getDeviceForHttpRequest($_
SERVER);
}

// store session data $_SESSION['wurflData']=$requestingDevice;

$_SESSION['modernizrData']=$_POST['modernizrData'];

$i = 0;

$capabilities = $requestingDevice->getAllCapabilities();
$countCapabilities = count($capabilities);
```

```php
?>
{
  "wurflData": <?php

    //echo json_encode($capabilities);
    foreach(array_keys($capabilities) as $capabilityName){
      $capability = $requestingDevice->getCapability($capabilityName);
      $isString = true;
      if($capability == "true" ||
         $capability == "false" ||
         is_numeric($capability))
      {
        $isString = false;
      }

      echo "\"".$capabilityName
        ."\":".(($isString)?"\"":"")1
        .$requestingDevice->getCapability($capabilityName)
        .(($isString)?"\"":"");

      if(($i + 1) < $countCapabilities){
        echo ",\n";
      }

      $i++;
    }
  ?>
}
```

 This example has commented out the easy way of JSON encoding an associative array. Replacing that is some PHP code that will send back JSON encoding that uses real Boolean and numeric values instead of storing everything as a string.

With these files, you now know everything that can be known about your visitors on both the server side and client side.

Mobilizing full-site pages – the hard way

Why would we do it the hard way? Why? Really there's only one good reason: to keep the content on the same page so that the user doesn't have one page for mobile and one page for desktop. When e-mails and tweets and such are flying around, the user generally doesn't care if they're sending out the mobile view or the desktop view and they shouldn't. As far as they're concerned, they're sending content to someone. This is one of the prime arguments for responsive design. But don't worry, we'll take this this into consideration later when we do things the easy way too.

Generally, it's pretty easy to tell what parts of a site would translate to mobile. Almost regardless of the site layout there are data attributes you'll be throwing onto existing tags to mobilize them. When jQuery Mobile's libraries are not present on the page, these attributes will simply sit there and cause no harm. Then you can use one of our many detection techniques to decide when to throw the jQM libraries in.

Know your role

Let's consider some of key data-role attributes that are needed to mobilize a page:

- `data-role="page"`: This contains everything that will show in the mobile view.

- `data-role="header"`: This wraps h1, h2, h(x), and up to two links in the appearance of a bar and turns the links into buttons. You can put more into a header but it's not advisable. If you've got that much to try to squeeze into the header, you might be better off having a single "Menu" button. Header bars can have their positions fixed. Anything within the header bar will remain fixed at the top.

- `data-role="content"`: This provides a margin around your content.

- `data-role="button"`: This turns a link into a button.

- `data-role="navbar"`: This creates a navbar when wrapped around a list of links.

- `data-role="footer"`: This wraps anything you want at the bottom. It's a great place for secondary links, next-step navigation, contact us, and all that legal stuff that signals the end of all usefulness. This can also be given a fixed position.

- `data-role="none"`: This prevents jQuery Mobile from styling the content.

From an ideal user experience perspective, pages would contain nothing more than what was necessary for the user to accomplish the task for which they came to that page. *Let us have a moment of silence for the dream lost…* With that in mind, remember that anything inside of `data-role="page"` will show up on the mobile view. So, the best thing you can do on most full-site pages is to determine which chunk of the page the user actually came for, tag that section with a role of `content`, and then immediately wrap that with a tag whose role is `page`. In so doing, you will automatically cut out the rest of the cruft that fills the rest of most web pages.

Step 1 of 2 – focus on content, marketing cries foul!

At this point anyone with a marketing background might be crying foul because this approach cuts out their messaging and targeted advertising and such. However, it is worth noting that people have had the ability to do this very thing on their own for a while now. Controversial services such as Pocket (formerly known as Read it Later), Instapaper, and even the simple Reader tool on iOS Safari are providing the user with exactly what they want. Here is an example of a normal desktop site on the left and how the iOS Reader strips away everything but the content itself:

We have a choice; provide the user with what they want in the format they want or possibly lose the chance to reach them at all as they turn to such tools. This will require a more creative approach to marketing activities on mobile. But make no mistake, ejecting everything else but the core of the page should be your first step.

After gutting everything but the main content of the page, we'll also need to gut the styles and scripts that are currently in the head. If we have access to modify the page itself we can easily do this on the server side using WURFL. Otherwise, we could always use JavaScript to remove the stylesheets and scripts we don't want and then inject ours. We could also simply highjack the first stylesheet and then remove the rest and do the same with the scripts to first bring in jQuery and then jQuery Mobile. There are a thousand ways to tackle the situation but I'd really recommend using WURFL if you're going to mobilize an existing page in this fashion. Otherwise, it's just going to get messy.

Step 2 of 2 – choose global navigation style and insert

So, at this point, we've got the beginnings of the page but there may still be some minor things that need removing. Having a mobile stylesheet to take care of those few overrides will be quite helpful and quicker than cleaning up with JavaScript DOM manipulation. That's pretty simple, the next big question is, how do we deal with the global navigation since we just explicitly excluded it.

Global nav as a separate page

This is probably the simplest approach and keeps the interface as clean as possible (mentioned in the following steps):

1. Wrap the global nav in its own separate roles of page and content and be sure they're easily selectable.

2. At the bottom of the page (or really anywhere after the global nav and content are complete) put in a script that moves the containing page of global nav below the content. This is particularly important because we are now in a multipage view and the first "page" in the DOM will be shown to the user when jQuery Mobile kicks in. We want to do this before jQuery Mobile even knows it should do anything. If we don't, the user who came to the site expecting to read something will first be greeted by a global nav. Here is a very simple example based on the pages we previously saw:

    ```
    $("#NavMainC").insertAfter("#ContentW");
    ```

3. Append headers to these internal pages so they can link to each other:

```
$("#ContentW").prepend("<div data-role='header'><h3>"+$("title").
text()+"</h3><a href='#NavMainC' data-icon='grid' class='ui-btn-
right'>Menu</a></div>")

$("#NavMainC").prepend("<div data-role='header'><a data-rel='back'
data-icon='back' href='javascript://'>Back</a><h3>Menu</h3></a>");
```

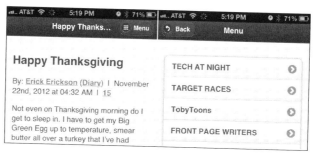

Global nav at the bottom

In pages such as articles where the user is likely to read all the way to the bottom, it is not uncommon to put the menu at the bottom of the page. It's an approach that fosters continued engagement. They're already there, right? Perhaps you might throw a link to a related article or two and then append the global menu to the bottom of the page. This would give the user something more to read without having to scroll all the way back to the top:

Personally, I think it's best to take this two-pronged approach. The menu at the top links to the bottom and the menu at the bottom includes a link to return to the top. This is accomplished by the `$.mobile.silentScroll` function.

Global nav as a panel

As of jQuery 1.3 there is now a `Panel` component that can be embedded directly into a page and then revealed by button click. It's exactly like the Facebook app:

This is probably the simplest approach to global navigation. It also has the benefit of not changing pages or cluttering the interface. For the full API and options around the new panel widget, check out `http://view.jquerymobile.com/1.3.0/docs/widgets/panels/`.

The hard way – final thoughts

All in all, the approach of injecting attributes into a full-site page and invoking jQuery Mobile can work pretty well. The biggest problem that you will encounter is the sheer amount of cruft that is thrown onto most pages. There's a lot to remove and/or CSS-out. This also has the unfortunate effect of being rather brittle. If somebody comes along and even slightly modifies the page, it could break your implementation. I could really only recommend this approach if the pages are created using a template or a **content management system (CMS)** so that changes to the site structure won't happened often and will be uniform when they do.

Mobilizing full-site pages – the easy way

There is nothing easier and cleaner than just creating a standalone jQuery Mobile page. Let's just do that and simply import the page we want with AJAX. We can then pull out the parts we want and leave the rest.

The biggest disadvantage to this approach is mostly academic. Progressive enhancement is shot. The site completely breaks for anyone who doesn't have JavaScript on their device. My contention is that it probably doesn't matter. I can't speak for everywhere, but here in the United States, if you're not on a smartphone, you're not on the web with your device. Simple as that. There are of course exceptions that only prove the rule. However, if your market is different, you would want to consider if this option is right for you. So, let's continue.

On any given page, all we'll really need is a simple redirect for anyone on mobile using one of the many methods we've laid out. Then, just use a simple `location.replace`. This code sample does a little more than that. It checks to see if the user was on a mobile and clicked the full-site link. If so, we'll insert an `iframe` tag to allow the user to switch back to the mobile view manually. Otherwise, we're just going to bounce them to the mobile view:

```
if (isMobile && isSmallScreen) {
  if (document.cookie.indexOf("mobileFullSiteClicked=") < 0) {
    location.replace("mobileadapter.php?p="
      +escape(location.pathname));
  } else {
    document.addEventListener("DOMContentLoaded", function() {
      try {
        var iframe = document.createElement("iframe");
        iframe.setAttribute("src","gomo.html");
        iframe.setAttribute("width","100%");
        iframe.setAttribute("height","80");
        document.body.insertBefore(
          iframe,
          document.body.firstChild);
      } catch(e) {alert(e);}
    }, false);
  }
}
```

Here is the code for a page to allow the full site to link back into mobile. This file is `gomo.html` within the chapter code files:

```
<!doctype html>
<html>
<head>
  <meta charset="UTF-8">
  <style type="text/css">
    body{ background-color:#000;}
    p{
      font-size:60px;
```

```
        font-family:Arial, Helvetica, sans-serif;
        text-align:center;
      }
      a{color:white;}
    </style>
  </head>
  <body>
  <script type="text/javascript">
    document.write("<p><a href='mobileadapter.php?p="
      +escape(window.parent.location.pathname)
      +"' target='_top'>Switch to mobile view</a>"
      +"<img src='32-iphone@2x.png'/></p>");
  </script>
  </body>
  </html>
```

These two pages are both using scripts that do not require jQuery. It sure would be nice if every page had jQuery but there are competing platforms out there and we can't count on the base page that we're mobilizing to have it ready for us. Native JavaScript is faster anyway. We can put it right at the top of the page without having to pull in a library first.

Here is the jQuery Mobile page that houses the mobilized content. It also links back to the full site view and sets a cookie so the user doesn't just get bounced back to mobile if they click on the full-site link.

As mentioned earlier, we're pulling in the next top 3 articles and placing them before the menu at the bottom to keep the user engaged. It's far easier to do in this view.

The example also takes advantage of `replaceState`. For all browsers that support it, when the user comes to the mobile page, the URL in the address bar and history will be updated to show the URL of the original article.

Now, without further delay, we will now see the best example of how to easily mobilize full-site pages. It is generic enough that you could probably just take this to whatever project you're working on and only have to tweak the code that's doing the pulling and injection:

```html
<!DOCTYPE html>
<html>
<head>
  <meta charset="utf-8">
  <meta name="viewport" content="width=device-width, initial-scale=1">
  <title class="pageTitle">Loading...</title>
  <link rel="stylesheet" href="http://code.jquery.com/mobile/1.3.0/
jquery.mobile-1.3.0.min.css" />
  <script src="http://code.jquery.com/jquery-1.8.2.min.js"></script>
  <script src="http://code.jquery.com/mobile/1.3.0/jquery.mobile-
1.3.0.min.js"></script>
  <!-- cookie code from https://github.com/carhartl/jquery-cookie -->
  <script src="jquery.cookie.js"></script>
  <style type="text/css">
    #iscfz,.comment-bubble{display:none;}
    #bottomMenu .byline
    {
      padding:0 0 8px 12px;
      font-weight:normal;
    }
  </style>
</head>
<body>
<div id="mainPage" data-role="page">
```

This section is the new panel available in jQuery Mobile 1.3. It will receive the global menu:

```html
    <div data-role="panel" id="globalmenu" data-position="left"
data-display="reveal" data-theme="a">
    <ul data-role="listview"></ul>
    <!-- panel content goes here -->
  </div><!-- /panel -->
```

```
<div data-role="header">
  <a href="#globalmenu" data-icon="bars">Menu</a>
  <h1 class="pageTitle">Loading...</h1>

</div><!-- /header -->
<div id="mainContent" data-role="content">
</div><!-- /content -->
<div>
  <ul id="bottomMenu" data-role="listview"></ul>
</div>
<div data-role="footer">
  <h4>
    <a class="fullSiteLink" data-role="button" data-inline="true"
href="<?php echo htmlspecialchars(strip_tags($_REQUEST["p"])) ?>"
target="fullsite">Full Site View</a>
  </h4>
</div><!-- /footer -->
</div><!-- /page -->

<script type="text/javascript">

  $.cookie("mobileFullSiteClicked","true", {
    path:"/",expires:0}
  );  //0 minutes - erase cookie
```

What we're doing here to replace the state in the users history is not fully supported by all mobile browsers. Just to be on the safe side, I've wrapped that line in a try/catch block. This is a good technique for anything that has partial support across your customer base.

```
try{
    //make the URL the original URL so if the user shares
    //it with others, they'll be sent to the appropriate URL
    //and that will govern if they should be shown
    //mobile view.
    history.replaceState({},"","<?php echo htmlspecialchars(strip_
tags($_REQUEST["p"])) ?>");
  }catch(e){
    //history state manipulation is not supported
  }

  //Global variable for the storage of the imported
  //page content. Never know when we might need it
  var $pageContent = null;
```

```
//Go get the content we're supposed to show here
function loadPageContent(){

    $.ajax({
        //strip_tags and htmlspecialchars are to to help
        //prevent cross-site scripting attacks
        url:"<?php echo htmlspecialchars(strip_tags($_REQUEST["p"]))
?>",

        beforeSend: function() {
          //show the page loading spinner
          $.mobile.loading( 'show' );
        }
    })
    .done(function(data, textStatus, jqXHR){

        //jQuery the returned page and thrown it into
        //the global variable
        $pageContent = $(data);

        //take the pieces we want and construct the view
        renderPage();
    })
    .fail(function(jqXHR, textStatus, errorThrown){

        //let the user know that something went wrong
        $("mainContent").html("<p class='ui-bar-e'>Aw snap! Something
went wrong:<br/><pre>"+errorThrown+"</pre></p>");
    })
    .always(function(){
        //Set a timeout to hide the image, in production
        //it was being told to hide before it had even been shown
        //resulting a loading gif never hiding
        setTimeout(function(){$.mobile.loading( "hide" )}, 300);
    });;
}
```

This next section takes care of pulling apart the imported page and injecting it to the right places. Note at the beginning where I'm selecting objects and using a dollar sign at the beginning of the name. We preselect them for the sake of performance. Anything you're going to reference more than once should be stored to a variable to reduce DOM traversal to select it again. The reason for the dollar sign is that it indicates to the coder that the variable they're looking at has already been jQueried:

```
function renderPage(){
  var $importedPageMainContent = $pageContent.find("#main");
  var $thisPageMainContent = $("#mainContent");

  //pull the title and inject it.
  var title = $importedPageMainContent.find("h1.title").text();

  $(".pageTitle").text(title);

  //set the content for the main page starting
  //with the logo then appending the headline,
  //byline, and main content
  var $logo = $pageContent.find("#logo-headerC img");

  $thisPageMainContent.html($logo);
  $thisPageMainContent.append(
    $importedPageMainContent.find("h1.title")
  );
  $thisPageMainContent.append(
    $importedPageMainContent.find("div.byline")
  );
  $thisPageMainContent.append(
    $importedPageMainContent.find("div.the-content")
  );

  var $bottomMenu = $("#bottomMenu");

  //Take the next 3 top stories and place them in the
  //bottom menu to give the user something to move on to.
  $bottomMenu.html("<li data-role='list-divider'>Read On...</li>");
  $bottomMenu.append(
    $pageContent.find("#alldiaries li:lt(3)")
  );

  //Inject the main menu items into the bottom menu

  $bottomMenu.append("<li data-role='list-divider'>Menu</li>");

  var $mainMenuContent = $pageContent.find("#NavMain");
  $bottomMenu.append($mainMenuContent.html());

  //After doing all this injection, refresh the listview
  $bottomMenu.listview("refresh");

  //inject the main menu content into main menu page
  var $mainMenContent = $("#mainMenuContent");
  $mainMenContent.find("ul").append(
    $mainMenuContent.html()
  );
```

```
}

//once the page is initialized, go get the content.
$("[data-role='page']").live("pageinit", loadPageContent);
//if the user clicks the full site link, coolie them
//so they don't just bounce back.
$("a.fullSiteLink").live("click", function(){
  $.cookie("mobileFullSiteClicked","true",
    {path:"/",expires:30});  //30 minutes
});

</script>
</body>
</html>
```

 The cookie management that is being used here comes from the jQuery cookie plugin at `https://github.com/carhartl/jquery-cookie`.

Summary

Earlier in this book we looked at mobile detection in depth. Now you know all there is to know. Before, we were creating mobile sites from scratch with little care what their desktop experiences were. Now you know how to unify them. The hard part is knowing when to craft mobile experiences from scratch and when to simply mobilize the full-site experience. It's a pity there's no simple answer to that. But, whether by using JavaScript on page to manipulate it into mobile (the hard way) or by AJAXing in the content and picking the pieces you want (the easy way) or by leveraging responsive design + server side components (RESS) as we mentioned in the previous chapter, you're ready to handle virtually every possible situation now. The only thing we haven't really tackled yet is integrating with a CMS which we'll do in the next chapter.

9
Content Management Systems and jQM

"I am a web developer. It is a waste of my time and talent to take a Microsoft Word document and cut and paste content to a web page every time the client wants a change" — Overheard everywhere, countless times.

If this statement resonates within you, then you need to be familiar with content management systems (CMS). They're an easy and powerful way to put publishing power in your users' hands so that you can focus on less tedious, better paying work. All you have to do is help the client set up their CMS, choose and customize their templates, and leave the content creation and maintenance to them. CMS is often at the core of both small business websites and corporate websites.

For the popular platforms, there are *many* plugins and themes to choose from. Brochureware sites have never had it so easy. In fact, platforms like WordPress and Squarespace are making this process so easy that often a web developer is not needed for anything more than customizing the look and feel.

So, why even include this chapter? Because the popularity of CMS almost always guarantees that if you're going to be making mobile web apps, at one point or another you're going to get a client that already has a site in a CMS, and you need to know how to integrate.

In this chapter, we will cover:

- The current CMS landscape
- WordPress and jQuery Mobile
- Drupal and jQuery Mobile
- Updating your WordPress and Drupal themes
- Adobe Experience Manager (AEM)

The current CMS landscape

WordPress is the world's most popular CMS, by volume. For the top 10,000 websites, 8.3 percent are built on WordPress. The next highest is Drupal, with 2.95 percent. Granted that doesn't sound like much, but look at this chart from `http://trends.builtwith.com/cms`. Among all the sites that use a CMS, WordPress and Drupal account for almost 75 percent.

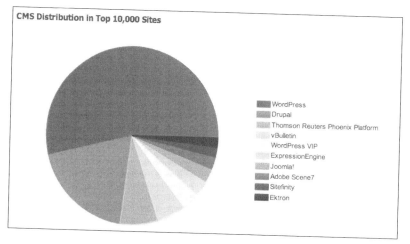

WordPress and jQuery Mobile

WordPress is popular because it's easy and user friendly. You can get started with WordPress by creating a hosted site on `WordPress.com`, or you can download the source and install it on any machine you like by going to `WordPress.org`. While you're experimenting, I would highly recommend the latter approach. The version used in this chapter is 3.5.

The key to getting up and running quickly with any CMS is, realizing which plugins and themes to use. For WordPress, I would *not* recommend a jQuery Mobile plugin. As I was experimenting for this chapter, it broke the admin interface and was, in general, a miserable experience. However, there are several jQuery Mobile themes that will serve you well. Some are free, some paid. Either way, try not to reinvent the wheel. Pick a theme that is closest to what you want and then tweak it. Chances are, by now, you're more than good enough to modify existing theme files. Here are the links to some themes I found and liked. Pick one, unzip it, and put it in your WordPress install directory under `wp-content/themes/`:

- `http://www.mobilizetoday.com/freebies/jqmobile`
- `http://themeforest.net/item/mobilize-jquery-mobile-wordpress-theme/3303257`

- `http://goldenapplesdesign.com/projects/jquery-mobile-boilerplate-for-wordpress-themes/`(my personal favorite)

Mac tip

Open the console, navigate to the folder that contains your unzipped directories, and run the following command. If you don't, your stuff might not show up or work as expected.

`xattr -dr com.apple.quarantine *`

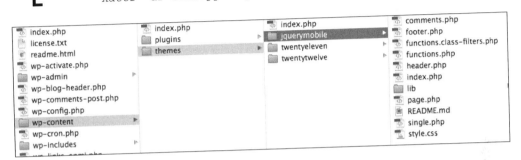

If you've successfully installed the theme, you should be able to view it on the admin interface under **Appearance | Themes**, as shown on the left-hand side of the next image. It should be listed under **Available Themes**:

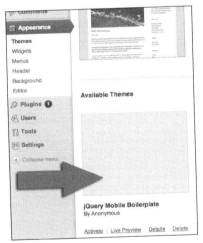

Next, we'll need a way to access the theme on mobile devices. That's where the mobile theme switcher comes in. The switcher we'll use here is simple but effective for the vast majority of people who are likely to visit your site.

Manually installing the mobile theme switcher

To manually install the mobile theme, download it from `http://wordpress.org/extend/plugins/mobile-theme-switcher/`. Unzip the folder and put it in your WordPress install directory under `wp-content/plugins/`:

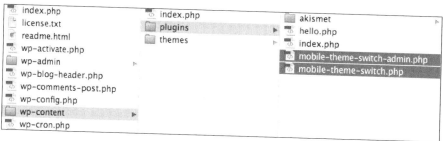

Next, through the admin interface, activate the plugin titled **Mobile theme switch**:

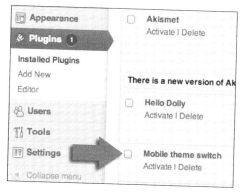

Automatically installing the mobile theme switcher

You can let WordPress do most of the work for you if you like. Personally, I like taking control of things. Here's how you can install it through the admin interface:

1. Go to the **Plugins** page and then look beside the title to find the **Add new** button, as shown in the next screenshot:

2. On the following screen, search for **mobile theme switcher**:

3. There are plenty of options to choose from, the one we're using is the first:

4. Enter your FTP credentials on the next page.

5. Activate your newly installed plugin.

Configuring the mobile theme switcher

If you have successfully installed and activated the plugin, it will now show up under the **Appearance** menu, as shown in the following screenshot. Then, select the mobile theme you installed and click on the **Update Options** button:

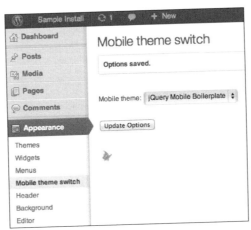

The combination of the plugin and theme is powerful, simple, and effective. Here is a screenshot of the new theme in action:

Pretty simple, eh? Now, we just have to tweak it till the client is content. Let's move on to the next CMS system.

Drupal and jQuery Mobile

Drupal is a far more powerful CMS. Using some of their standard plugins, you can easily create full blown web apps, not just brochureware sites. You want to use CAPTCHA for people to prove they're human before posting comments? There's a plugin for that. Want to create a contact form? It's built-in. Want to create a custom database table and form to save that input? As of Drupal 7, that's built-in as well.

The biggest downside to Drupal is that it has a bit of a learning curve if you want to tap its true power. Also, without some tuning, it can be a little slow and can really bloat your page's code. Techniques like caching can improve performance but can also negatively impact dynamically created pages.

Configuring Drupal for jQuery Mobile is an almost identical process to that of WordPress. Again, we'll start with a theme that already exists. The people who've made these themes know the system they're coding for. Don't try to reinvent the wheel. All we have to do is use the theme and tweak it. My favorite jQM theme for Drupal can be found at `http://drupal.org/project/mobile_jquery`. At the bottom of that page, you will find the downloadable distributions for the theme:

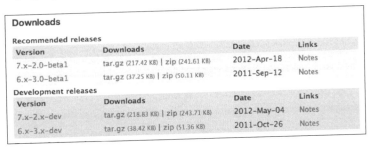

1. Copy the link to the distribution that's right for you.

2. Log in to the admin console of your Drupal site and go to the **Appearance** section:

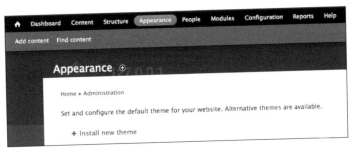

3. Click on the **Install new theme** link and paste the link you copied into the **Install from a URL** field. Click on the **Install** button and let the installation go through all its steps.

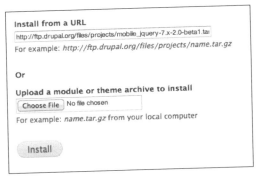

4. Chances are that at this point, you won't be able to see the installed theme. The makers encourage you to create subthemes and not use their base installation for the theme. This is one recommendation we'll be ignoring. So, in order to make the theme show up, you'll want to edit the file `mobile_jquery.info` in `sites/all/themes/jquery_mobile/` in your Drupal install directory and change the value of `hidden` from `1` to `0`. Once you do that, you should see the theme listed in the disabled themes section of the **Appearance** menu, as show in the next screenshot. Click on the **Enable** link, and your theme will be ready to be configured and used.

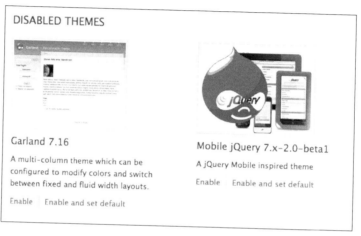

5. Next, we have to install the theme switcher plugin. Let's use the plugin at `http://drupal.org/project/mobile_theme`. Again, choose the right version and copy its URL.

Downloads

Recommended releases

Version	Downloads	Date	Links
7.x–1.2	tar.gz (8.78 KB)	zip (9.77 KB)	2011–May–02	Notes

Development releases

Version	Downloads	Date	Links
7.x–1.x–dev	tar.gz (8.78 KB)	zip (9.77 KB)	2011–Mar–26	Notes
6.x–1.x–dev	tar.gz (6.79 KB)	zip (7.45 KB)	2011–Feb–25	Notes
5.x–1.x–dev	tar.gz (6.77 KB)	zip (7.43 KB)	2011–Feb–25	Notes

6. Open the admin interface to the **Modules** section and click on the **Install new module** link:

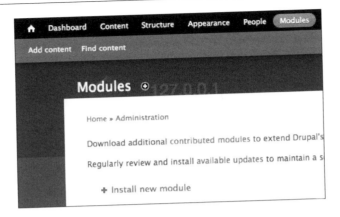

7. Paste the URL into the field labeled **Install from a URL** and click on the **Install** button. Let the installation process run its course.

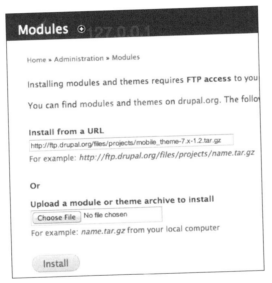

8. At the bottom of the **Modules** section, you will find the newly installed plugin:

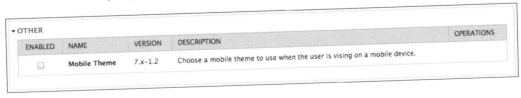

9. Click on the checkbox to enable the module and then you'll be able to configure it:

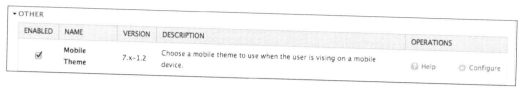

10. Clicking on the **Configure** link will take you to a screen for configuring the **Global settings**. On the right-hand side of that screen, you will find a section for configuring the mobile theme options. The **Mobile theme** section has been marked with a red arrow in the following screenshot:

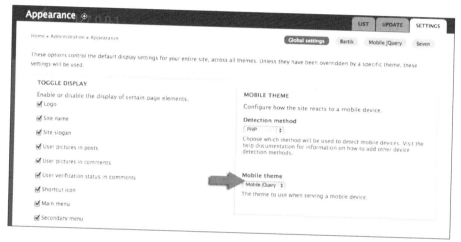

The results speak for themselves. The theme could certainly use customization, but it works just fine for a start. We know how to do the rest.

Updating your WordPress and Drupal templates

At some point (probably right after the installation), you'll want to update these themes to use the latest versions of the jQuery Mobile library. Some are still using the beta version. The process is actually pretty straightforward. All you have to do is find the header sections of the templates in question, and update the references to the jQuery Mobile CSS, JS, and probably the core jQuery library.

WordPress – Golden Apples jQM Theme

For the WordPress theme by Golden Apples (see `https://github.com/goldenapples/jqm-boilerplate`), you're going to have to change several files. In the `header.php` file, find and update the following line:

```
<link rel="stylesheet" href="http://code.jquery.com/mobile/1.0b1/
jquery.mobile-1.0b1.min.css" />
```

In the `functions.php` file, you'll need to find and update the following lines:

```
wp_enqueue_script( 'jquery',
                    "http://code.jquery.com/jquery-1.6.4.min.js" );

wp_enqueue_script( 'jquery-mobile',
"http://code.jquery.com/mobile/1.0.1/jquery.mobile-1.0.1.min.js",
array( 'jquery' ) );

wp_enqueue_script( 'mobile-scripts',
get_stylesheet_directory_uri().'/lib/mobile-scripts.js', array(
'jquery', 'jquery-mobile' ) );

wp_localize_script( 'mobile-scripts', 'siteData', array(
'siteUrl', home_url() ) );

wp_enqueue_style( 'jquery-mobile',
"http://code.jquery.com/mobile/1.0.1/jquery.mobile-1.0.1.min.css"
);
```

Drupal – jQuery Mobile Theme

For the Drupal jQuery Mobile theme at `http://drupal.org/project/mobile_jquery`, the quickest way for you to update the theme is to edit the `template.php` file at the root of the `theme` folder. Find the following lines in the file and update the references to jQuery Mobile:

```
drupal_add_css('http://code.jquery.com/mobile/1.0.1/jquery.mobile.
structure-1.0.1.min.css', array_merge($css_options,
 array('weight' => 100)));
```

```
drupal_add_css('http://code.jquery.com/mobile/1.0.1/jquery.mobile-
1.0.1.min.css', array_merge($css_options,
array('weight' => 100)));

drupal_add_js('http://code.jquery.com/jquery-1.6.4.min.js',
array_merge($js_options, array('weight' => 100)));

drupal_add_js(drupal_get_path('theme', 'mobile_jquery') . '/scripts/
mobile_jquery.js', array_merge($js_options,
array('weight' => 101)));

drupal_add_js('http://code.jquery.com/mobile/1.0.1/jquery.mobile-
1.0.1.min.js', array_merge($js_options, array('weight' => 101)));
```

Adobe Experience Manager

Adobe has always been a leader in the web space. Their premier corporate CMS is called Adobe Experience Manager (AEM) (see `http://www.adobe.com/solutions/web-experience-management.html`). I'm not going to get into how to install, configure, or code for AEM. That is a subject for several training manuals the size of this book. Trust me. I am only mentioning this so you know that there is at least one major CMS player that comes with complete jQuery Mobile examples.

The training materials are centered on a fictional site called Geometrixx.

The beauty of the AEM system is that it uses a Java JCR container (see `http://en.wikipedia.org/wiki/Content_repository_API_for_Java`) to store content. This means that you can create mobile sites that automatically pull content from desktop pages simply by referencing the JCR content nodes of the desktop pages or by allowing users to type directly into an interface that looks like a mobile screen.

The mobile example of Geometrixx is coded using jQuery Mobile; while the version of jQM is a bit outdated, it's easy to change the templates. The mobile content author interface comes with simulated phone interfaces to frame the content so it looks roughly like it would on a real phone or tablet. You can switch device profiles right in the author interface. While this is not a true simulation of those devices since it's all taking place in whatever browser you're using, it is still very, very handy.

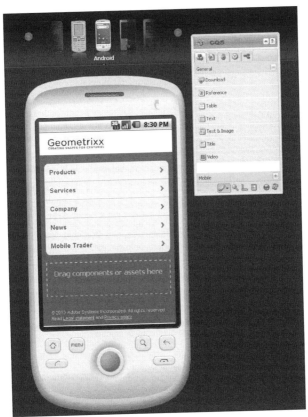

If you work for a company that can afford AEM, you'll already be well-versed in the mobile implementation. The power this platform gives to content authors is astounding.

Summary

The world of mobile themes has exploded since I first started dipping into mobile development two years ago. Today, there are lots of options for jQuery Mobile; there are also some other responsive themes. I didn't bother making an exhaustive list of everything that Google can give us. By the time this book is published, that will have changed, even in the space of a month. The important thing to remember is that we don't have to reinvent the wheel, and we don't have to saddle ourselves with content updates. Give your clients the power to make minor updates themselves, and you get back to the business of your business. As useful as CMS is, we won't be covering it again. The next chapter will be a return to custom development, where we'll combine everything we've learned so far.

10
Putting It All Together – Flood.FM

Flood.FM is a unique idea. This is a website where listeners will be greeted with music from local, independent bands across several genres and geographic regions. Building this will take many of the skills we've developed so far, and we'll pepper in some new techniques that can be used in this new service. We've already drawn interfaces on Post-its, and used GPS and client-side templates. We've taken care of regular HTML5 audio and video. We've even started working on multiple mobile sizes and used media queries to rework our layouts into responsive designs.

All of these were simpler implementations meant to get the job done and be as gracefully failing as possible. Let's see what technology and techniques we could bring to bear on this venture.

In this chapter we will cover:

- A taste of Balsamiq
- Organizing your code
- Introduction to the Web Audio API
- Prompting the user to install your app
- New device-level hardware access
- To App or not to App, that is the question
- PhoneGap versus Apache Cordova

A Taste of Balsamiq

We started this book by learning a technique called paper prototyping. For your own work with clients, it's a great tool. However, if you're dealing with larger or distributed teams, you might need something more. Balsamiq (`http://www.balsamiq.com/`) is a very popular UX tool for rapid prototyping. It is perfect for creating and sharing interactive mockups.

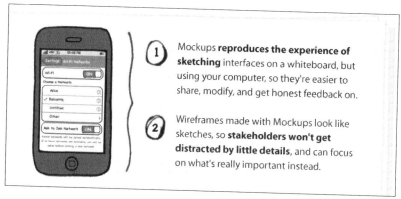

1. Mockups **reproduces the experience of sketching** interfaces on a whiteboard, but using your computer, so they're easier to share, modify, and get honest feedback on.

2. Wireframes made with Mockups look like sketches, so **stakeholders won't get distracted by little details,** and can focus on what's really important instead.

And when I say very popular, I mean lots of major names that you're used to seeing. Over 80,000 companies create their software with the help of Balsamiq Mockups.

So, let's take a look at what the creators of Flood.FM had in mind. Here is the first screen they drew; it looks like a pretty standard implementation so far. It has an icon toolbar at the bottom and a listview in the content. Translating that is pretty simple, really. We've done this before using Glyphish icons and standard toolbars.

Ideally, we'd like to keep this particular implementation as pure HTML/JS/CSS. That way, we could compile it into a native app at some point using PhoneGap. However, we'd like to stay true to the DRY (Don't Repeat Yourself) principle. That means that we're going to want to inject this footer onto every page without using a server-side process. To that end, let's set up a hidden part of our app to contain all the global elements that we may want:

```html
<div id="globalComponents">
  <div data-role="navbar" class="bottomNavBar">
    <ul>
      <li><a class="glyphishIcon" data-icon="notes" href="#stations_
by_region" data-transition="slideup">stations</a></li>
      <li><a class="glyphishIcon" data-icon="magnify" href="#search_
by_artist" data-transition="slideup">discover</a></li>
      <li><a class="glyphishIcon" data-icon="calendar" href="#events_
by_location" data-transition="slideup">events</a></li>
      <li><a class="glyphishIcon" data-icon="gears" href="#settings"
data-transition="slideup">settings</a></li>
    </ul>
  </div>
</div>
```

We'll keep this code at the bottom of the page and hide it with a simple CSS rule in the stylesheet, `#globalComponents{display:none;}`.

Now let's set up our application to insert this global footer into each page, just before they are created. Using the `clone()` method (shown in the next code snippet) ensures that not only are we pulling over a copy of the footer, but also any data attached with it. In this way, each page is built with the exact same footer, just like it is in a server-side include. When the page goes through its normal initialization process, the footer will receive the same markup treatment as the rest of the page.

```javascript
/***********************
 *  The App
 ***********************/
var floodApp = {
  universalPageBeforeCreate:function(){
    var $page = $(this);
    if($page.find(".bottomNavBar").length == 0){
      $page.append($("#globalComponents .bottomNavBar").clone());
    }

  }
}
```

```
/************************
*   The Events
***********************/
//Interface Events
$(document).on("pagebeforecreate", "[data-role="page"]",floodApp.
universalPageBeforeCreate);
```

Look at what we've done here in this piece of JavaScript code. It's a little different from what we've done before. We're actually organizing our code a little more effectively.

Organizing your code

In the previous chapters, we structured our code very loosely. In fact, I'm sure the academic types would laugh at the audacity of even calling it structured. I believe in a very pragmatic approach to coding, which leads me to use more simple structures and a bare minimum of libraries. However, there are values and lessons to be learned out there.

MVC, MVVM, MV*

For the last couple of years, serious JavaScript developers have been bringing backend development structures to the web as the size and scope of their project demanded a more regimented approach. For highly ambitious, long-lasting, in-browser apps, this kind of structured approach can help. This is even more true if you're on a larger team.

MVC stands for "Model-View-Controller" (see `http://en.wikipedia.org/wiki/Model%E2%80%93view%E2%80%93controller`), **MVVM** is for "Model View ViewModel"(see `http://en.wikipedia.org/wiki/Model_View_ViewModel`), and **MV*** is shorthand for "Model View Whatever" and is the general term used to sum up this entire movement of bringing these kinds of structures to the front-end.

Some of the more popular libraries include:

- Backbone.JS (`http://backbonejs.org/`)
- Spine (`http://spinejs.com/`)
- Lumbar (`http://walmartlabs.github.com/lumbar/`)
- Ember (`http://emberjs.com/`)
- Knockout (`http://knockoutjs.com/`)
- AngularJS (`http://angularjs.org/`)
- Batman.js (`http://batmanjs.org/`)

A very nice comparison of these, and more, is at `http://codebrief.com/2012/01/the-top-10-javascript-mvc-frameworks-reviewed/`.

An adapter and sample of how to make Backbone play nicely with jQuery Mobile can be found at `http://view.jquerymobile.com/1.3.0/docs/examples/backbone-require/index.php`.

An example for Ember can be found at `https://github.com/LuisSala/emberjs-jqm`.

Angular also has adapters for jQM in progress. There are several examples at `https://github.com/tigbro/jquery-mobile-angular-adapter`.

MV* and jQuery Mobile

Yes, you can do it. You can add any one of these MV* frameworks to jQuery Mobile and make as complex an app as you like. Of them all, I lean toward the Ember platform for desktop and Angular for jQuery Mobile. However, I'd like to propose another alternative.

I'm not going to go in-depth into the concepts behind MVC frameworks. Essentially, it's all about separating the concerns of your application into more manageable pieces, each having a specific purpose. We don't need yet another library/framework to do this. It is simple enough to write code in a more organized fashion. Let's create a structure similar to what I've started before:

```
//JavaScript Document

/*******************
 * The Application
 ******************/


/*******************
 * The Events
 ******************/


/*******************
 * The Model
 ******************/
```

The application

Under the application section, let's fill in some of our app code and give it a *namespace*. Essentially, namespacing is taking your application-specific code and putting it into its own named object so that the functions and variables won't collide with other potential global variables and functions. It keeps you from polluting the global space and helps preserve your code from those who are ignorant regarding your work. Granted, this is JavaScript and people can override anything they wish. However, this also makes it a whole lot more intentional to override something like `floodApp.getStarted` than simply creating your own function called `getStarted`. Nobody is going to accidentally override a namespaced function.

```
/*********************
 * The application
 *********************/
var floodApp = {
  settings:{
    initialized:false,
    geolocation:{
      latitude:null,
      longitude:null,
    },
    regionalChoice:null,
    lastStation:null
  },
  getStarted:function(){
    location.replace("#initialize");
  },
  fireCustomEvent:function(){
    var $clicked = $(this);
    var eventValue = $clicked.attr("data-appEventValue");
    var event = new jQuery.Event($(this).attr("data-appEvent"));
    if(eventValue){ event.val = eventValue; }
    $(window).trigger(event);
  },
  otherMethodsBlahBlahBlah:function(){}
}
```

Pay attention, in particular, to the function `fireCustomEvent`. With that, we can now set up an event management system. At its core, the idea is pretty simple. We'd like to be able to simply put tag attributes on our clickable objects and have them fire events, like all the MV* systems. This fits the bill perfectly. It would be quite common to set up a click event handler on a link or something to catch the activity. This is far more simple. Just an attribute here and there, and you're wired in. The HTML code becomes more readable too. It's easy to see how declarative this makes your code:

```
<a href="javascript://" data-appEvent="playStation" data-appEventValue
="country">Country</a>
```

The events

Now instead of watching for clicks, we're listening for events. You can have as many parts of your app as you like registering themselves to listen for the event and then execute appropriately.

As we fill out our application more and more, we'll start collecting a lot of events; instead of letting them get scattered throughout multiple nested callbacks and such, we'll be keeping them all in one handy spot. In most JavaScript MV* frameworks, this part of the code is referred to as the Router. Hooked to each event, you will see nothing but namespaced application calls:

```
/*******************
 * The events
 *******************/

//Interface events
$(document).on("click", "[data-appEvent]",
   floodApp.fireCustomEvent);
$(document).on("pagebeforeshow",
   "[data-role="page"]",floodApp.universalPageBeforeShow);

$(document).on("pagebeforecreate",
   "[data-role="page"]",floodApp.universalPageBeforeCreate);

$(document).on("pageshow", "#initialize",
   floodApp.getLocation);

$(document).on("pagebeforeshow", "#welcome",
   floodApp.initialize);

//Application events
$(window).on("getStarted",
   floodApp.getStarted);
$(window).on("setHomeLocation",
   floodApp.setHomeLocation);
$(window).on("setNotHomeLocation",
   floodApp.setNotHomeLocation);
$(window).on("playStation",
   floodApp.playStation);
```

Notice the separation of concerns into interface events and application events. We're using this as a point of distinction between events that are fired as a result of natural jQuery Mobile events (interface events) and events that we have thrown (application events). This may be an arbitrary distinction, but for someone who comes along later to maintain your code, this could come in handy.

The model

The model section contains the data for your application. This is typically the kind of data that is pulled in from your backend APIs. It's probably not as important here, but it never hurts to namespace what's yours. Here, we have labeled our data as `modelData`. Any information we pull in from the APIs can be dumped right into this object, like we've done here with the station data:

```
/*******************
 * The Model
 *******************/
var modelData = {
  station:{
    genres:[
        {
          display:"Seattle Grunge",
          genreId:12,
          genreParentId:1
        }
    ],
    metroIds[14,33,22,31],
    audioIds[55,43,26,23,11]
  }
}
```

Pair this style of programming with client-side templating, and you'll be looking at some highly maintainable, well-structured code. However, there are some features that are still missing. Typically, these frameworks will also provide bindings for your templates. This means that you only have to render the templates once. After that, simply updating your model object will be enough to cause the UI to update itself.

The problem with these bound templates is that they update the HTML in a way that would be perfect for a desktop application. But remember, jQuery Mobile does a lot of DOM manipulation to make things happen.

In jQuery Mobile, a listview starts like this:

```
<ul data-role="listview" data-inset="true">
  <li><a href="#stations">Local Stations</a></li>
</ul>
```

After the normal DOM manipulation, you get this:

```
<ul data-role="listview" data-inset="true" data-theme="c"
style="margin-top:0" class="ui-listview ui-listview-inset ui-corner-
all ui-shadow">
  <li data-corners="false" data-shadow="false" data-iconshadow="true"
```

```
data-wrapperels="div" data-icon="arrow-r" data-iconpos="right" data-
theme="c" class="ui-btn ui-btn-icon-right ui-li-has-arrow ui-li ui-
corner-top ui-btn-up-c">
<div class="ui-btn-inner ui-li ui-corner-top">
<div class="ui-btn-text">
<a href="#stations" class="ui-link-inherit">
Local Stations
</a>
</div>
<span class="ui-icon ui-icon-arrow-r ui-icon-shadow"> </span>
</div>
</li>
</ul>
```

And that's just a single list item. You really don't want to include all that junk in your templates; so what you need to do is, just add your usual items to the listview and then call `.listview("refresh")`. Even if you're using one of the MV* systems, you'll still have to either find or write an adapter that will refresh the listviews when something is added or deleted. With any luck, these kinds of things will be solved at the platform level soon. Until then, using a real MV* system with jQM will be a pain in the posterior.

Introduction to the Web Audio API

When we touched upon the subject of HTML audio in *Chapter 6, HTML5 Audio*, we were looking at it from a perspective of progressive enhancement and maximum device support. We took regular pages with native audio controls and used JavaScript to build a new interface to control the audio. We then looked at ways to combine it all and go for the better experience. Now we'll take it a few steps further.

The Web Audio API is a fairly new development and, at the time of writing this, only existed within the mobile space on iOS 6. The Web Audio API is available on the latest versions of desktop Chrome, so you can still do your initial test coding there.

For now, this means no Android, no Windows Phone, and no Blackberry. At least, not yet. However, it's only a matter of time before this is built into other major platforms.

Most of the code for this part of the project and the full explanation of the API can be found at `http://developer.apple.com/library/safari/#documentation/AudioVideo/Conceptual/Using_HTML5_Audio_Video/PlayingandSynthesizingSounds/PlayingandSynthesizingSounds.html`.

Let's use feature detection to branch our capabilities:

```
function init() {
if("webkitAudioContext" in window) {
    myAudioContext = new webkitAudioContext();
    // ananalyser is used for the spectrum
    myAudioAnalyser = myAudioContext.createAnalyser();
    myAudioAnalyser.smoothingTimeConstant = 0.85;
    myAudioAnalyser.connect(myAudioContext.destination);

    fetchNextSong();
} else {
    //do the old stuff
}
}
```

The original code for this page was designed to kick off simultaneous downloads for every song in the queue. With a fat connection, this would probably be OK. Not so much on mobile. Because of the limited connectivity and bandwidth, it would be better to just chain the downloads to ensure better experience and a more respectful use of bandwidth:

```
function fetchNextSong() {
var request = new XMLHttpRequest();
  var nextSong = songs.pop();
  if(nextSong){
    request = new XMLHttpRequest();
    // the underscore prefix is a common naming convention
    // to remind us that the variable is developer-supplied
    request._soundName = nextSong;
    request.open("GET", PATH + request._soundName + ".mp3",
              true);
    request.responseType = "arraybuffer";
    request.addEventListener("load", bufferSound, false);
    request.send();
  }
}
```

Now the `bufferSound` function just needs to call `fetchNextSong` after buffering, as shown in the following code snippet:

```
function bufferSound(event) {
  var request = event.target;
  var buffer = myAudioContext.createBuffer(
  request.response, false);
  myBuffers.push(buffer);
  fetchNextSong();
}
```

One last thing we need to change from the original is, telling the buffer to pull the songs in the order that they were inserted:

```
function playSound() {
    // create a new AudioBufferSourceNode
    var source = myAudioContext.createBufferSource();
    source.buffer = myBuffers.shift();
    source.loop = false;
    source = routeSound(source);
    // play right now (0 seconds from now)
    // can also pass myAudioContext.currentTime
    source.noteOn(0);
    mySpectrum = setInterval(drawSpectrum, 30);
    mySource = source;
}
```

For anyone on iOS, this solution is pretty nice. There is a lot more to this API for those who want to dig in. With this out-of-the-box example, you get a nice canvas-based audio analyzer that gives you a very nice professional look as the audio levels bounce to the music. Slider controls are used to change the volume, the left-right balance, and the high-pass filter. If you don't know what a high-pass filter is, don't worry, I think that filter's usefulness went the way of the cassette deck. Regardless, it's fun to play with.

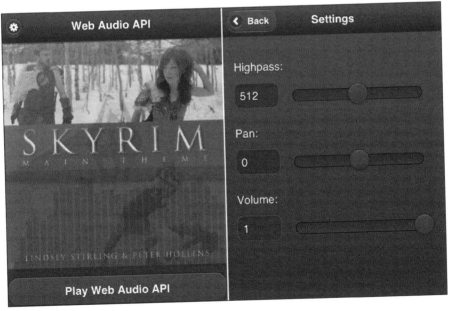

The Web Audio API is a very serious piece of business. This example was adapted from the example on Apple's site. It only plays one sound. However, the Web Audio API was designed with the idea of making it possible to play multiple sounds, alter them in multiple ways, and even dynamically generate sounds using JavaScript. Getting that deep is probably worth a book of its own. It would also require a deeper knowledge of audio processing than I am likely to ever have. In the meantime, if you want to see this proof of concept in jQuery Mobile, you will find it in the example source in `webaudioapi.html`. For an even deeper look at what is coming, you can check the docs at `https://dvcs.w3.org/hg/audio/raw-file/tip/webaudio/specification.html`.

Prompting the user to install your app

Remember in *Chapter 6, HTML5 Audio*, we added the Apple touch icons to make the Lindsey Stirling site look like an app when bookmarked to the home screen? We even went so far as to use a manifest file to locally cache the assets for faster access and offline use.

Now let's take a look at how we can prompt our users to download the Flood.FM app to their home screens. It is very likely that you've seen it before; it's the little bubble that pops up and instructs the user with the steps to install the app.

There are many different projects out there, but the best one that I have seen is a derivative of the one started by Google. Much thanks and respect to Mr. Okamototk on GitHub (`https://github.com/okamototk`) for taking and improving it. Okamototk evolved the bubble to include several versions of Android, legacy iOS, and even BlackBerry. You can find his original work at `https://github.com/okamototk/jqm-mobile-bookmark-bubble`. However, unless you can read Japanese or enjoy translating it, I'd recommend you just take the code from this chapter's example.

Don't worry about annoying your customers too much. With this version, if they dismiss the bookmarking bubble three times, they won't see it again. The count is stored in HTML5 LocalStorage; so if they clear out the storage, they'll see the bubble again. Thankfully, most people out there don't even know that can be done, so it won't happen very often. Usually it's geeks like us that clear things like LocalStorage and cookies, and we know what we're getting into when we do it.

In my edition of the code, I've combined all the JavaScript into a single file meant to be placed between your import of jQuery and jQuery Mobile. At the top, the first non-commented line is:

```
page_popup_bubble="#welcome";
```

This is what you would change to be your own first page or where you want the bubble to popup.

In my version, I have hardcoded the font color and text shadow properties into the bubble. This was needed because in jQM, the font color and text shadow color vary based on the theme you're using. Consequently, in jQuery Mobile's default "A" theme (white text on a black background), the font was showing up as white with a dark shadow on top of a white bubble. Now, with my modified version for jQM, it will always look right.

We just need to be sure we've set up our page with the proper links in the head, and that our images are in place:

```
<link rel="apple-touch-icon-precomposed" sizes="144x144" href="images/
album144.png">
<link rel="apple-touch-icon-precomposed" sizes="114x114" href="images/
album114.png">
<link rel="apple-touch-icon-precomposed" sizes="72x72" href="images/
album72.png">
<link rel="apple-touch-icon-precomposed" href="images/album57.png">
<link rel="shortcut icon" href="img/images/album144.png">
```

Note the Flood.FM logo here. The logo is pulled from our link tags marked with `rel="apple-touch-icon-precomposed"` and injected into the bubble. So, really, the only thing in `jqm_bookmark_bubble.js` that you would need to alter is `page_popup_bubble`.

New device-level hardware access

New kinds of hardware-level access are coming to our mobile browsers every year. Here is a look at some of what you can start doing now and what's on the horizon. Not all of these are applicable to every project but if you think creatively, you can probably find innovative ways to use them.

Accelerometers

Accelerometers are the little do-dads inside your phone that measure the phone's orientation in space. To geek out on this, read `http://en.wikipedia.org/wiki/Accelerometer`.

This goes beyond the simple orientation we've been using. This is true access to the accelerometers, in detail. Think about the user being able to shake their device or tilting it as a method of interaction with your app. Maybe Flood.FM is playing something they don't like and we can give them a fun way to rage against the song. Something like, "shake a song to never hear it again." Here is a simple marble rolling game somebody made as a proof of concept. See `http://menscher.com/teaching/woaa/examples/html5_accelerometer.html`.

Camera

Apple's iOS 6 and Android's JellyBean can both access photos on their file systems as well as the cameras. Granted, these are the latest and greatest versions of these two platforms. If you intend to support the many woefully out of date Android devices (2.3 2.4) that are *still* being sold off the shelves as if brand new, then you're going to want to go with a native compilation like PhoneGap or Apache Cordova to get that capability.

```
<input type="file" accept="image/*">
<input type="file" accept="video/*">
```

The following screenshot has iOS to the left and Android to the right:

APIs on the horizon

Mozilla is doing a lot to push the mobile web API envelope. Here is what is now on the horizon and will probably be ready to use in less then two years:

- battery levels
- charging status
- ambient light sensors
- proximity sensors
- vibration
- contacts
- network information
- mobile connection (carrier, signal strength, and so on)
- Web SMS
- Web Bluetooth
- Web FM
- Archive API (opening and reading contents from compressed folders)

If you want to read more, check out `https://wiki.mozilla.org/WebAPI`.

To app or not to app, that is the question

Should you or should you not compile your project into a native app? Here are some things to consider.

Raining on the parade (take this seriously)

When you compile your first project into an app, there is a certain thrill that you get. You did it! You made a real app! It is at this point that we need to remember the words of Dr. Ian Malcolm from the movie Jurassic Park (Go watch it again. I'll wait):

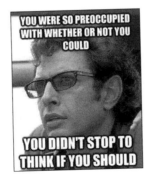

"You stood on the shoulders of geniuses to accomplish something as fast as you could, and before you even knew what you had, you patented it, and packaged it, and slapped it on a plastic lunchbox, and now [bangs on the table] you're selling it, you wanna sell it. Well... your scientists were so preoccupied with whether or not they could that they didn't stop to think if they should."

These words are very close to prophetic for us. In the end, their own creation ate most of the guests for lunch.

According to this report from August 2012 http://www.webpronews.com/over-two-thirds-of-the-app-store-has-never-been-downloaded-2012-08 (and several others like it that I've seen before), *over two-thirds of all apps on the app stores have never been downloaded.* Not even once! So, realistically, app stores are where most projects go to die.

Even if your app is discovered, the likelihood that anyone will use it for any significant period of time is astonishingly small. According to this article in Forbes (http://tech.fortune.cnn.com/2009/02/20/the-half-life-of-an-iphone-app/), most apps are abandoned in the space of minutes and never opened again. Paid apps last about twice as long, before either being forgotten or removed. Games have some staying power, but let us be honest, jQuery Mobile isn't exactly a compelling gaming platform, is it?

The Android world is in terrible shape. Devices can still be purchased running ancient versions of the OS, and carriers and hardware partners are not providing updates to them in anything even resembling a timely fashion. If you want to monitor the depths of sorrow that could be yours by embracing a native strategy, look here:

http://developer.android.com/about/dashboards/index.html

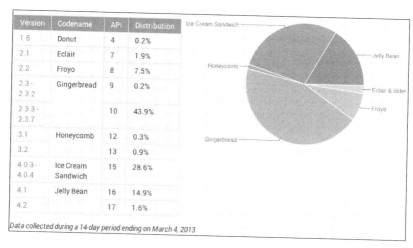

Version	Codename	API	Distribution
1.6	Donut	4	0.2%
2.1	Eclair	7	1.9%
2.2	Froyo	8	7.5%
2.3 - 2.3.2	Gingerbread	9	0.2%
2.3.3 - 2.3.7		10	43.9%
3.1	Honeycomb	12	0.3%
3.2		13	0.9%
4.0.3 - 4.0.4	Ice Cream Sandwich	15	28.6%
4.1	Jelly Bean	16	14.9%
4.2		17	1.6%

Data collected during a 14-day period ending on March 4, 2013

You can see just how fractured the Android landscape is as well as how many older versions you'll probably have to support. Until Android and its business partner pull their collective heads out, Android will continue to be the Internet Explorer 6 of the native mobile world. You do *not* want to support that.

On the flip side, if you're publishing strictly to the web, then every time your users visit your site, they'll be on the latest edition using the latest APIs, and you'll never have to worry about somebody using some out-of-date version. Do you have a security patch you need to apply? You can do it in seconds. If you're on the Apple app store, this patch could take days or even weeks.

Three good reasons for compiling an app

Yes, I know I just finished telling you about your slim chances of success and the fire and brimstone you will face for supporting apps. However, here are a few good reasons to make a real app. In fact, in my opinion, they're the only acceptable reasons.

The project itself IS the product

This is the first and only sure sign that you need to package your project as an app. I'm not talking about selling things through your project. I'm talking about the project itself. It should be made into an app. May the force be with you.

Access to native-only hardware capabilities

GPS and camera are reliably available for the two major platforms in their latest editions. iOS even supports accelerometers. However, if you're looking for more than this, you'll need to compile down to an app to get access to these APIs.

Push notifications

Do you like them? I don't know about you, but I get way too many push notifications; any app that gets too pushy either gets uninstalled or its notifications are completely turned off. I'm not alone in this. However, if you simply must have push notifications and can't wait for the web-based implementation, you'll have to compile an app.

Supporting current customers

OK, this one is a stretch, but if you work in corporate America, you're going to hear it. The idea is that you're an established business and you want to give mobile support to your clients. You or someone above you has read a few whitepapers and/or case studies that show that almost 50 percent of people search in the app stores first.

Even if that were true (which I'm still not sold on), you're talking to a businessperson. They understand money, expenses, and escalated maintenance. Once you explain to them the cost, complexity, and potential ongoing headaches of building and testing for all the platforms and their OS versions in the wild, it becomes a very appealing alternative to simply put out a marketing push to your current customers that you're now supporting mobile, and all they have to do is go to your site on their mobile device. Marketing folks are always looking for reasons to toot their horns at customers anyway. Marketing might still prefer to have the company icon on the customer's device to reinforce brand loyalty, but this is simply a matter of educating them that it can be done without an app.

You still may not be able to convince all the right people that apps are the wrong way to go when it comes to customer support. If you can't do it on your own, slap them on their heads with a little Jakob Nielson. If they won't listen to you, maybe they'll listen to him. I would defy anyone who says that the Nielsen Norman Group doesn't know what they're saying. See `http://www.nngroup.com/articles/mobile-sites-vs-apps-strategy-shift/`.

> *"Summary: Mobile apps currently have better usability than mobile sites, but forthcoming changes will eventually make a mobile site the superior strategy."*

So the $64,000 question becomes: are we making something for right now or for the future? If we're making it for right now, what are the criteria that should mark the retirement of the native strategy? Or do we intend to stay locked on it forever? Don't go into that war without an exit strategy.

PhoneGap versus Apache Cordova

Well, after all that, if you're still thinking of making a native app, I salute you. I admire your spirit and wish you the best of luck.

 If you Google "jquery mobile phonegap performance", you're going to find a *lot* of negative articles. The problems seem legion. Sluggish performance, screen blinking between transitions, and so on. Not that Sencha Touch or any other mobile web frameworks seem to be doing any better. Just be aware that it may not perform as well as it would over the web.

PhoneGap started out as a project to take regular HTML, JS, and CSS and package them nicely into a distributable app for any app store. Eventually, it became part of the Apache Software Foundation. At its core, PhoneGap *is* Apache Cordova. In fact, if you go the documentation site for Cordova, it's actually still hosted at `http://docs.phonegap.com/`.

In addition to simply compiling down your app, you also get access to the following device-level APIs.:

- Accelerometer: Tap into the device's motion sensor.
- Camera: Capture a photo using the device's camera.
- Capture: Capture media files using the device's media capture applications.
- Compass: Obtain the direction that the device is pointing to.
- Connection: Quickly check the network state and cellular network information.
- Contacts: Work with the device's contacts database.
- Device: Gather device-specific information.
- Events: Hook into native events through JavaScript.
- File: Hook into native file systems through JavaScript.
- Geolocation: Make your application location-aware.
- Globalization: Enable representation of objects specific to a locale.
- InAppBrowser: Launch URLs in another in-app browser instance.
- Media: Record and play back audio files.
- Notification: Visual, audible, and tactile device notifications.
- Splashscreen: Show and hide the applications splash screen.
- Storage: Hook into the device's native storage options.

So far, so good. We get a lot more stuff we can do, and we can do it all in JavaScript.

Next, we need to actually build our app. You'll need to download PhoneGap or Cordova onto your machine. Don't forget to download the SDKs for every platform you intend to support as well. No, wait, scratch that!

Now there is PhoneGap Build. It's a cloud-based build service for PhoneGap. You don't have to install any SDKs at all. PhoneGap Build just took all the work out of this. If you want it to compile iOS apps, you'll still to provide them with your developer certificates, but aside from that little hiccup, you're good to go.

To get started, all you have to do is log in with either your Adobe ID or your GitHub ID. Then either paste in the URL to the GitHub repo you want to build, or upload a zip file less than 9.5 MB in size:

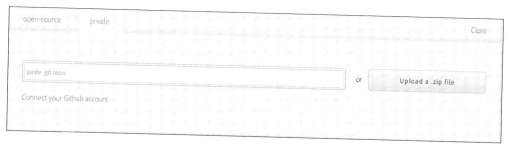

Next, you fill out a little information about the app itself:

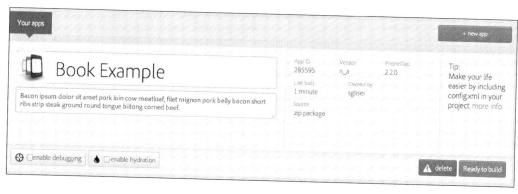

Click on the **Ready to build** button. Now just sit back and watch the pretty progress spinners do their thing.

Look, they even give you a lovely little QR code to scan for downloading the app. The only reason it's giving a red symbol on iOS is because, at this point, I have not given them my developer certificates.

Summary

I don't know about you, but I'm exhausted. I really don't think there's any more that can be said about jQuery Mobile or its supporting technologies at this time. You've got examples on how to build things for a whole host of industries, and ways to deploy it through either the Web or PhoneGap Build. At this point, you should be quoting Bob the Builder. "Can we build it? Yes, we can!"

I hope this book has assisted and/or inspired you to go make something great. I hope you change the world and get filthy stinking rich doing it. I'd love to hear your success stories as you move forward. To let me know how you're doing, or to let me know of any errata, or even if you just have some questions, please don't hesitate to email me directly at shane@roughlybrilliant.com. Now, go be brilliant!

Index

Symbols

$.mobile.changePage function 113
$.mobile.silentScroll function 186

A

Adobe CQ 206, 207
AngularJS 212
Apache Cordova
  versus PhoneGap 226-228
app compilation
  conditions 223-226
app installation
  prompting, by user 220, 221
Apple 10
Axure RP 19

B

Backbone.JS 212
background images
  cycling 166-168
Balsamiq 210, 211
Balsamiq Mockups 19
Batman.js 212
bufferSound function 218
buttons 32

C

client-side templating 102, 103
clone() method 211
CMS 187, 195
code
  organizing 212

code organization

code organization
  application 214
  events 215
  jQuery Mobile 213
  model 216
  MV* 213
  MVC 212
  MVVM 212
Configure link 204
content management system. See CMS
cURL 108
current CMS landscape 196
custom CSS 42
custom fonts
  web font providers 37, 38
custom icons
  defining 32, 34

D

data-icon attribute 32
data-url attribute 57
desktop-sized devices 166
device-level APIs 227
directions-panel attribute 89
document.location function 57
DOM weight management 113, 114
Drupal
  about 200
  and jQuery mobile 200
  jQuery mobile 200-204
Drupal templates
  jQuery Mobile Theme 205
  updating 205

E

e-commerce tracking
Google Analytics, using 72, 73
emails
linking to 34, 37
Ember 212

F

FDS 18
final product 41
fireCustomEvent function 214
fixed position toolbars 128, 129
Fonts.com Web Fonts 37
Font Squirrel 37
footer attribute 89
full code 170
full-site pages
global nav 185, 186
global nav, as panel 187
global navigation style, choosing 185
mobilizing 183-194
Functional Design Spec. *See* **FDS**

G

gallery screen
design concepts 159-161
generated pages 113, 114
geolocation 77-87
geolocation.getCurrentPosition function 83
Geometrixx 206, 207
GitHub 220
global CSS 28
global JavaScript
about 26
.live 27
.on 27
Glyphish 32, 34
Google Analytics
used, for e-commerce tracking 72, 73
Google Feeds API
leveraging 122-124
Google Maps API
about 87
integrating 88-92

Google Static Maps
about 53-55
Google Analytics, adding 55-59
Google Web Fonts 37
GPS monitoring 92, 95

H

home screen
saving, HTML5 manifest used 150-152
href element 34
HTML
breaking, into server side template 29-31
HTML5 Audio
about 126, 128
controlling, JavaScript used 130-135
in iOS 136
HTML5 Audio all-in one
solution 136-140, 142, 149
HTML5 manifest
used, for home screen saving 150-152
HTML5 Web Storage
about 119
browser-based databases 120
JSON 120
HTML prototyping
about 11
paper-based ideation 11, 12

I

icons 32
Indexed Database 120
Install new theme link 201
iOS
HTML5 Audio 136

J

JavaScript
used, for HTML5Audio controlling 130-135
jQuery mobile
and Drupal 201-204
jQuery Mobile. *See* **jQM**
jQM
about 196
page change programatically 113

jQuery Mobile boilerplate
  about 21, 22
  full-site links 24, 25
  meta viewport differences 23, 24
jQuery Mobile elements
  drawing, ways 14, 15
jQuery Mobile Theme roller 24
jQuery Templates 103
jQuery Validate
  integrating 62-72
JSON 102
JSON APIs
  patching 104-111
JsRender 103

K

Knockout 212

L

LAMP 28
Linux, Apache, MySql, PHP. *See* LAMP
logo 32
long forms 60, 61
Lumbar 212

M

MAMP 173
map_canvas attribute 89
max-width property 119
meta.php file 69
meta viewport tag 23
mobile device detect
  browser sniffing 172
  feature detection 172
  JavaScript-based browser sniffing 177, 178
  JavaScript-based feature detection,
      Modernizr used 178, 179
  JavaScript-based lean feature detection 179
  Server-side plus client-side
      detection 179-182
  WURFL 172-177
mobile theme switcher
  automatic installation 198, 199
  configuring 199, 200
  manual installation 198

Model-View-Controller. *See* MVC
Model View ViewModel *See* MVVM
Model View Whatever *See* MV*
multi-page forms 60, 61
MV* 212
MVC 212
MVVM 212

N

navbar attribute 89
navigator.geolocation.watchPosition
      method 92
new device-level hardware access
  accelerometers 222
  APIs 223
  camera 222

O

optimization
  about 39
  tips 39-41

P

page curl shadow effects
  list items 38
pageshow event 136
paper prototyping
  alternates, Axure RP 19
  alternates, Balsamiq Mockups 19
PhoneGap
  versus Apache Cordova 226-228
PhotoSwipe
  basic gallery, creating 154-156
  URL 154
Plugins page 198

Q

QR codes
  about 76
  generating 77
  using 76, 77

R

Ready to build button 229
required function 63
Require.js 39
responsive design 162-164
Responsive Design + Server Side
    Components. *See* RESS
Responsive web design. *See* RWD
RESS 169
resulting first page 47, 48
RSS feeds
    leveraging 114-118
    responsive images, forcing 119
RWD 156-161

S

searchTerm attribute 110
site
    buttons 32
    creating, need for 31
    customer testimonials 32
    custom icons, defining 32
    Glyphish 32
    icons 32
    logo 32
small business
    Call buttons 16
    Map It button 15
    site setting 15-18
    starting with 12-14
smart phone-sized devices 164
SPDY protocol 39
Spine 212

T

tablet-sized devices 165
ThemeRoller 155
TypeKit 37

U

user
    detecting, JavaScript used 49, 50
    detecting on server 51
    getting, to mobile site 48, 49
    redirecting, JavaScript used 49, 50
User experience (UX) 10

V

validateMe class 78
validate options 63
validator methods 63
video
    embeddding 99, 100
    linking 98-100

W

Web Audio API 217-220
Web SQL Database 120
WordPress
    about 196
    Golden Apples jQM Theme 205
WordPress templates
    updating 205
WURFL 51, 169

X

XAMPP 173

Thank you for buying
Creating Mobile Apps with jQuery Mobile

About Packt Publishing

Packt, pronounced 'packed', published its first book "*Mastering phpMyAdmin for Effective MySQL Management*" in April 2004 and subsequently continued to specialize in publishing highly focused books on specific technologies and solutions.

Our books and publications share the experiences of your fellow IT professionals in adapting and customizing today's systems, applications, and frameworks. Our solution based books give you the knowledge and power to customize the software and technologies you're using to get the job done. Packt books are more specific and less general than the IT books you have seen in the past. Our unique business model allows us to bring you more focused information, giving you more of what you need to know, and less of what you don't.

Packt is a modern, yet unique publishing company, which focuses on producing quality, cutting-edge books for communities of developers, administrators, and newbies alike. For more information, please visit our website: www.packtpub.com.

About Packt Open Source

In 2010, Packt launched two new brands, Packt Open Source and Packt Enterprise, in order to continue its focus on specialization. This book is part of the Packt Open Source brand, home to books published on software built around Open Source licences, and offering information to anybody from advanced developers to budding web designers. The Open Source brand also runs Packt's Open Source Royalty Scheme, by which Packt gives a royalty to each Open Source project about whose software a book is sold.

Writing for Packt

We welcome all inquiries from people who are interested in authoring. Book proposals should be sent to author@packtpub.com. If your book idea is still at an early stage and you would like to discuss it first before writing a formal book proposal, contact us; one of our commissioning editors will get in touch with you.

We're not just looking for published authors; if you have strong technical skills but no writing experience, our experienced editors can help you develop a writing career, or simply get some additional reward for your expertise.

jQuery Mobile Web Development Essentials

ISBN: 978-1-84951-726-3   Paperback: 246 pages

Learn to use the touch-optimized, cross-device, cross-platform jQM web framework for smartphones and tablets

1. Create websites that work beautifully on a wide range of mobile devices with jQuery mobile

2. Learn to prepare your jQuery mobile project by learning through three sample applications

3. Packed with easy to follow examples and clear explanations of how to easily build mobile-optimized websites

jQuery Mobile Cookbook

ISBN: 978-1-84951-722-5   Paperback: 320 pages

Over 80 recipes with examples and practical tips to help you quickly learn and develop cross-platform applications with jQuery Mobile

1. Create applications that use custom animations and use various techniques to improve application performance

2. Use and customize the various controls such as toolbars, buttons, and lists with custom icons, icon sprites, styles, and themes

3. Write simple but powerful scripts to manipulate the various configurations and work with the events, methods, and utilities which are provided by the framework

Please check **www.PacktPub.com** for information on our titles

Made in the USA
San Bernardino, CA
05 June 2013